Raw Faith Bible Study

Raw Faith

kasey van norman

what happens when
God picks a fight

Leader's
Guide
Included

Bible Study

Tyndale House Publishers, Inc.

Carol Stream, Illinois

Visit Tyndale online at www.tyndale.com.

Visit Kasey Van Norman's website at www.kaseyvannorman.com.

TYNDALE and Tyndale's quill logo are registered trademarks of Tyndale House Publishers, Inc.

Raw Faith Bible Study: What Happens When God Picks a Fight

Designed by Jacqueline L. Nuñez

Edited by Stephanie Rische

Published in association with literary agent Jenni Burke of D. C. Jacobson and Associates, an author management company, www.DCJacobson.com.

Printed in the United States of America

ISBN 978-1-4143-6479-7

20   19   18   17   16   15
7   6   5   4   3   2

Contents

Before You Get Started

I'm not sure what your perspective is on God right now, but I'd like to assure you: he's a lot bigger than any of us even imagine him to be.

I'm not sure why you're doing this study—whether your friend talked you into it or you feel guilty about your lack of Bible reading or you're looking for something to kick-start you out of the spiritually dry place you've been in. Whatever the case, I believe we're ultimately here for the same reason: God wants to draw us closer to him and teach us something about faith over the next six weeks.

So here we are. You and me—complete and utter screwups, despite our best efforts otherwise. We're trying to be faithful even when we're unsure of our faith. Trying to be steady even when we're drowning in uncertainty. Trying to live well, even when we feel like giving up.

Where are you right now, dear reader? What if the past 365 days were a miniature lifetime, set apart for you to examine yourself? Have you lived well? Have you kept the faith? Have you run the race?

Wherever you find yourself on this journey of faith, you aren't where you need to be. Neither am I. In fact, none of us are. I'm here on this journey with you—not because it's easy or fun, but out of my desire to obey God.

My prayer is that by the end of this study, God will have transformed our hearts. I pray that we'll be unwilling to settle for anything less than complete and total transformation and that we will engage the very depths of our souls—the places that have been squashed by life and damaged beyond recognition. I pray that we will allow God's light to break the silence and darkness of the trenches we crawl into when we don't want the world to see how broken and foolish and messed up we truly are.

Sometimes truth burns like a fire, but that pain is the good kind, the productive kind. When it comes to faith, the truth will no doubt cause us mighty discomfort as the flesh and muscle and bone of our hearts are laid bare before his glory. But it's actually a good thing when the raw places of who we think we are and what we think we know about our Creator are torn to shreds. Because only then can we see that his truth is the one ointment that can truly heal us.

May we be willing to empty everything before him over these next several weeks—our illnesses, our betrayals, our unforgiving hearts, our addictions, our depression, our insecurity, our pride, our money, our complacency, our damage, our stupidity, our brokenness, our small-mindedness. As we ponder faith in its purest, most organic, most vulnerable form, may his very Word come alive before our eyes.

And by the end of this season of study, may we raise our voices in victory, seeing that in his mercy, God is opening a new year, a new time, a new way of existing. May we desire Christ in all things—in the wounding and in the healing. May we triumph with hearts that renounce Satan's power and fight with a faith that goes beyond words, beyond comprehension.

Welcome to raw faith.

How to Use This Study

There is not one moment in our lives that takes place without first passing through the fingertips of our almighty Creator, and these moments you'll spend in Bible study are no different. I believe that, despite my own shortcomings and yours as well, the God of the universe has divinely appointed these weeks of study to change us, grow us, and water the dry, cracked soil of our faith. I beg you not to take this moment lightly. One day you and I will stand before God and answer to him for how we handled his Word. So let's make this moment in time count!

Whether you're doing this study as an individual on your lunch break or going through it alongside fellow faith diggers in a small group or studying it with a large class, these pages have been written with you in mind.

Before you begin, here are a few tools I'd like to make sure you have so you can get the most out of this study.

Raw Faith Leader's Guide

I'm always saying to myself, *Keep it simple, stupid.* So in honor of such grand words of wisdom (ha!), I've included the leader's guide for this study in the back of this book. If you complete this study in the context of a group, I recommend that you designate a leader, as this tends to keep the chaos to a minimum. Having held the role of small group leader before (with all the grace of a bull in a china closet), I know the comfort of having a warm blanket in the form of a leader's guide to cling to on lonely, dark nights.

If you are the lucky one nominated as leader, be sure to use the section at the back of this study to your full advantage. I've included notes about what to expect from this experience, pointers for leaders, group tips, and scheduling options.

Discussion/Reflection Questions

Note that I've included questions at the end of each week of this study. These questions are designed for either personal reflection or group discussion time. They can help you review what you've learned, clarify key truths, and give you some thoughts to ponder in the week ahead.

Raw Faith (The Book)

What's a cupcake without icing? Only half as good, if you ask me! If this Bible study is the cupcake, then the book is the icing (or perhaps it's the other way around, depending on who you ask). While this study can be used alone, it will be a fuller experience for you if you read them together. While the content is different, the themes overlap and are meant to be used in conjunction.

If you are serious about digging into real faith, I encourage you to work through this study alongside the book *Raw Faith*. In it I tell my personal story of finding out I had cancer, being faced with what faith really means in difficult times, and uncovering both my doubts about God and a deeper love for him. It was a season when everything I thought I knew about God, faith, others, and myself was squashed by chemotherapy, loneliness, and depression. But it was also the season God ultimately used to change the course of my life and my faith.

Other Resources

A Bible (duh!)

While my story might be captivating enough to change your mind, it will never have the power to change your heart. God's Word is the only tool that can even come close to making real, lasting, eternal changes where it matters—in your heart! I encourage you to never leave home without your Bible. And certainly don't start this study without one.

A journal and a pen

You'll need a pen to jot down your answers to the questions in this study. If you tend to write long answers or if you want to record your reflections in a more permanent place, you may want to keep a journal handy as well.

Note cards

You might want to get some note cards too—one of my personal favorite tools. This may sound simple and old school, but I find note cards work well for Scripture memorization. I encourage you to write down Scriptures that speak to you and bits of truth that jump off the page—you know, the ones that stick to your skin in a good way. Display these note cards on your fridge, on your dashboard, or on your mirror. Hey, I even have some taped to my shower door!

Week 1

A Raw Look at Faith

For most of my life, *faith* has been a word I kicked around when I couldn't really think of anything better to say.

"Why do you believe in God, Kasey?"

My response: "Well, because I have faith, of course."

"Kasey, what makes you sure you will get to heaven?"

My response: "My faith, of course."

Someone could have just as easily asked me, "Hey, Kasey, do you believe in rainbow-colored unicorns that shoot fairy dust from their backsides?" Because at that point, faith was just as far fetched and unrealistic as the notion of pixie-dust-snorting unicorns.

I knew the classic verse about faith in Hebrews 11:1: "Faith is being sure of what we hope for and certain of what we do not see" (NIV). But although I accepted it in theory, I never really dug deep and figured out what that would look like if I put it into practice in my own life.

What about you, my brave companion? Are you embracing a shallow, "safe" version of faith? Do you want to live out the full, abundant faith God has in mind for you?

Describe what comes to mind when you hear the word *faith*.

_____

_____

_____

_____

Why are you joining me on this crazy adventure toward raw faith?

_____

_____

_____

_____

Day 1

Both Christians and non-Christians can have a defective view of what the Christian life really is and what faith has to do with it. There are plenty of voices out there whispering lies to us about faith: the world, Satan, other people, and our own feelings. But God is an expert at blowing away the fog of confusion around us to show us who he really is and what his calling is for our lives.

Hebrews 11 is one of the clearest passages to help us brush away the cobwebs and get a sense of what real, authentic faith looks like. Let's take a look at Hebrews 11:29-38.

> It was by faith that the people of Israel went right through the Red Sea as though they were on dry ground. But when the Egyptians tried to follow, they were all drowned.
>
> It was by faith that the people of Israel marched around Jericho for seven days, and the walls came crashing down.
>
> It was by faith that Rahab the prostitute was not destroyed with the people in her city who refused to obey God. For she had given a friendly welcome to the spies.
>
> How much more do I need to say? It would take too long to recount the stories of the faith of Gideon, Barak, Samson, Jephthah, David, Samuel, and all the prophets. By faith these people overthrew kingdoms, ruled with justice, and received what God had promised them. They shut the mouths of lions, quenched the flames of fire, and escaped death by the edge of the sword. Their weakness was turned to strength. They became strong in battle and put whole armies to flight. Women received their loved ones back again from death.

But others were tortured, refusing to turn from God in order to be set free. They placed their hope in a better life after the resurrection. Some were jeered at, and their backs were cut open with whips. Others were chained in prisons. Some died by stoning, some were sawed in half, and others were killed with the sword. Some went about wearing skins of sheep and goats, destitute and oppressed and mistreated. They were too good for this world, wandering over deserts and mountains, hiding in caves and holes in the ground.

What miracles or unexplainable experiences take place in this passage?

_____

_____

What circumstances do the people in these verses experience?

_____

_____

How would you describe the faith of the people in this passage?

_____

_____

What did these people place their hope in during tough times?

_____

_____

What were these people of faith too good for?

_____

_____

For the men and women listed in Hebrews 11, life surely didn't turn out the way they'd expected. When children of God are permitted to experience suffering, rejection, and mistreatment, when children of God end up destitute and afflicted, we have trouble understanding what's happening. We think blessing follows faith, but blessing doesn't always look the way we think it will.

When faithful people suffer, God is ultimately giving a gift to the world. He is spreading his love and grace to the world through those who suffer and even die while clinging to the unshakable belief that the Lord is better than life itself.

Once upon a time, my aim was to live as comfortable a life as possible—to survive the brutal blows this world hands out with as little damage as possible and then move on. My goal was to wade in the shallow pool of contentment—go to church, have a loving husband and healthy children, get a house with a white picket fence and maybe a small dog, and above all to never venture far outside my religious box in my Southern Baptist small town, complete with sweet tea and steeples. I didn't want to look under the covers or ask questions that would stop preachers in their tracks or do anything to make waves.

But God wanted me to look closer. He invited me to dig deeper. With a single phone call and a dreaded diagnosis, I no longer had the option of shallow faith.

There's good news, though: it doesn't have to take a crisis for us to start embracing authentic faith. You can start living it today!

What is compelling to you about digging in and experiencing a deeper level of faith?

_____

_____

As you think about your life right now, what is holding you back from raw faith?

_____

_____

Day 2

During the two agonizing years I battled cancer, I experienced sides of God I never would have imagined. I saw him as my Provider, giving me the strength I needed to make it through each day. I saw him as my Father, gently caring for me when I was in pain. I saw him as my Friend, always near me when I was afraid and lonely. I saw him as my Redeemer, bringing good out of the worst circumstances. I saw him as the Lover of my soul—someone who loved me unconditionally, even when I had nothing to bring to the relationship. But I also experienced an aspect of God's character I'd never encountered before: God as a fighter.

And when I talk about God as a fighter, I'm not referring to God as one who fights for us, although he certainly does. In this case, I'm thinking more along the lines of a big guy in a boxing ring, a tough cage fighter, someone who lands a sucker punch in your gut out of nowhere.

Think of *that* guy.

Are you ticked off yet?

Good.

It may strike you as sacrilegious to talk about God as a fight picker—someone waiting to pounce when you least expect it. We've been taught that God is love and that he is a good Father—and he is all those things. But Scripture also makes it clear that sometimes God uses drastic measures to get our attention. In fact, some of God's greatest acts of love for us come through pain. Like a parent taking the training wheels off a child's bike or letting him fight his own battles, God knows that sometimes the most loving thing he can do is to let us fall down and get hurt.

Read the following passages and then write down what strikes you about God's
role in each passage.

> Oh, why give light to those in misery,
>> and life to those who are bitter?
> They long for death, and it won't come.
>> They search for death more eagerly than for hidden treasure.
> They're filled with joy when they finally die,
>> and rejoice when they find the grave.
> Why is life given to those with no future,
>> those God has surrounded with difficulties?
> I cannot eat for sighing;
>> my groans pour out like water.
> What I always feared has happened to me.
>> What I dreaded has come true.
> I have no peace, no quietness.
>> I have no rest; only trouble comes.
>
> JOB 3:20-26

_____

_____

> O LORD, how long will you forget me? Forever?
>> How long will you look the other way?
> How long must I struggle with anguish in my soul,
>> with sorrow in my heart every day?
> How long will my enemy have the upper hand?
>
> PSALM 13:1-2

_____

_____

> Without mercy the Lord has destroyed
>> every home in Israel.
> In his anger he has broken down
>> the fortress walls of beautiful Jerusalem.

He has brought them to the ground,
dishonoring the kingdom and its rulers.

All the strength of Israel
    vanishes beneath his fierce anger.
The Lord has withdrawn his protection
    as the enemy attacks.
He consumes the whole land of Israel
    like a raging fire.

He bends his bow against his people,
    as though he were their enemy.
His strength is used against them
    to kill their finest youth.
His fury is poured out like fire
    on beautiful Jerusalem.

Yes, the Lord has vanquished Israel
    like an enemy.
He has destroyed her palaces
    and demolished her fortresses.
He has brought unending sorrow and tears
    upon beautiful Jerusalem.

He has broken down his Temple
    as though it were merely a garden shelter.
The LORD has blotted out all memory
    of the holy festivals and Sabbath days.
Kings and priests fall together
    before his fierce anger.

LAMENTATIONS 2:2-6

_____

_____

Jesus said to his disciples, "If any of you wants to be my follower, you must turn from your selfish ways, take up your cross, and follow me. If you try to hang on to your life, you will lose it. But if you give up your life for my sake, you will save it."
MATTHEW 16:24-25

_____

_____

We think you ought to know, dear brothers and sisters, about the trouble we went through in the province of Asia. We were crushed and overwhelmed beyond our ability to endure, and we thought we would never live through it. In fact, we expected to die. But as a result, we stopped relying on ourselves and learned to rely only on God, who raises the dead.
2 CORINTHIANS 1:8-9

_____

_____

To me, living means living for Christ, and dying is even better.
PHILIPPIANS 1:21

_____

_____

Dear brothers and sisters, when troubles of any kind come your way, consider it an opportunity for great joy. For you know that when your faith is tested, your endurance has a chance to grow. So let it grow, for when your endurance is fully developed, you will be perfect and complete, needing nothing.
JAMES 1:2-4

_____

_____

This list only skims the surface of people in the Bible who got "beat up" and experienced suffering of some kind. In fact, if Scripture is any indication, suffering isn't the exception for believers; it seems to be the default. There's a long line of faithful followers of Christ who have gone before us and have the black eyes, broken bones, and bloody noses to show for it.

You probably won't like my saying this, but the truth is, God can be a bit of a bully. Now, he's not like your average school bully who gives you a wedgie and dunks your head in the toilet just for the sake of proving his power. God isn't like that. He does pick fights sometimes, but his motivation in doing so is always love.

From our limited human vantage point, we can't see the big picture, so what he's doing may not seem like love. But in the end, his love always shines through. Always.

Tell about a time you felt you were "sucker punched" by God. What happened? How did you respond to God in that moment?

_____

_____

_____

Read Genesis 32:22-32 for the account of Jacob's spiritual wrestling match.

During the night Jacob got up and took his two wives, his two servant wives, and his eleven sons and crossed the Jabbok River with them. After taking them to the other side, he sent over all his possessions.

This left Jacob all alone in the camp, and a man came and wrestled with him until the dawn began to break. When the man saw that he would not win the match, he touched Jacob's hip and wrenched it out of its socket. Then the man said, "Let me go, for the dawn is breaking!"

But Jacob said, "I will not let you go unless you bless me."

"What is your name?" the man asked.

He replied, "Jacob."

"Your name will no longer be Jacob," the man told him. "From now on you will be called Israel, because you have fought with God and with men and have won."

"Please tell me your name," Jacob said.

"Why do you want to know my name?" the man replied. Then he blessed Jacob there.

Jacob named the place Peniel (which means "face of God"), for he said, "I have seen God face to face, yet my life has been spared." The sun was rising as Jacob left Peniel, and he was limping because of the injury to his hip. (Even today the people of Israel don't eat the tendon near the hip socket because of what happened that night when the man strained the tendon of Jacob's hip.)

What did Jacob learn about God through this experience?

_____

_____

Have you ever felt like you were wrestling with God? What did you learn in the process?

_____

_____

Read 1 Peter 4:12-19.

Dear friends, don't be surprised at the fiery trials you are going through, as if something strange were happening to you. Instead, be very glad—for these trials make you partners with Christ in his suffering, so that you will have the wonderful joy of seeing his glory when it is revealed to all the world.

If you are insulted because you bear the name of Christ, you will be blessed, for the glorious Spirit of God rests upon you. If you suffer, however, it must not be for murder, stealing, making trouble, or prying into other people's affairs. But it is no shame to suffer for being a Christian. Praise God for the privilege of being called by his name! For the time has come for judgment, and it must begin with God's household. And if judgment begins with us, what terrible fate awaits those who have never obeyed God's Good News? And also,

"If the righteous are barely saved,
    what will happen to godless sinners?"

So if you are suffering in a manner that pleases God, keep on doing what is right, and trust your lives to the God who created you, for he will never fail you.

What are three truths we can learn about suffering from this passage?

_____

_____

Based on these words from 1 Peter, how should we respond when we feel like God is picking a fight with us?

_____

_____

Day 3

Let's begin today reading the following verses. As you read, look for the recurring theme that runs through each passage:

> Do you remember what I told you? "A slave is not greater than the master." Since they persecuted me, naturally they will persecute you. And if they had listened to me, they would listen to you.
>
> JOHN 15:20

> After preaching the Good News in Derbe and making many disciples, Paul and Barnabas returned to Lystra, Iconium, and Antioch of Pisidia, where they strengthened the believers. They encouraged them to continue in the faith, reminding them that we must suffer many hardships to enter the Kingdom of God.
>
> ACTS 14:21-22

> Everyone who wants to live a godly life in Christ Jesus will suffer persecution.
>
> 2 TIMOTHY 3:12

> Dear friends, don't be surprised at the fiery trials you are going through, as if something strange were happening to you.
>
> 1 PETER 4:12

Recurring theme:

_____

_____

For me the theme is simple: you'd better get ready. "Get ready for what?" you might ask. God wants us to get ready for suffering.

Suffering can come in many forms. It may come as a result of another person's sin or simply from living in a fallen world. We may suffer from grief, from a broken relationship with a loved one, from sickness, from financial strain, or from persecution that comes as a result of following Christ. When the things that give us security and enjoyment—money, reputation, health, children, self-esteem, relationships, success—are taken away, either by force or by choice, we suffer. Whatever the specific circumstances, we often find our faith shaken, and we ask, "How could you, God?"

Journal about a personal time of suffering—not just any suffering, but a time that caused you to wonder, *Why, God?*

_____

_____

_____

_____

The Bible is full of examples of people who suffered for a variety of reasons and in different ways. Here are just a few examples.

Read Job 1:13-19.

One day when Job's sons and daughters were feasting at the oldest brother's house, a messenger arrived at Job's home with this news: "Your oxen were plowing, with the donkeys feeding beside them, when the Sabeans raided us. They stole all the animals and killed all the farmhands. I am the only one who escaped to tell you."

While he was still speaking, another messenger arrived with this news: "The fire of God has fallen from heaven and burned up your sheep and all the shepherds. I am the only one who escaped to tell you."

While he was still speaking, a third messenger arrived with this news: "Three bands of Chaldean raiders have stolen your camels and killed your servants. I am the only one who escaped to tell you."

While he was still speaking, another messenger arrived with this news: "Your sons and daughters were feasting in their oldest brother's home. Suddenly, a powerful wind swept in from the wilderness and hit the house on all sides. The house collapsed, and all your children are dead. I am the only one who escaped to tell you."

What hardships did Job face?

_____

_____

Read Job 42:5.

I had only heard about you before,
    but now I have seen you with my own eyes.

After months of suffering, what does Job finally say to God?

_____

_____

Job was a godly, upright man who sought to please God. But he gained a new perspective on God in adversity that he never could have grasped in prosperity. The difference between how he saw God before and after his suffering was the difference between hearing and seeing.

Read Acts 6:8-15.

Stephen, a man full of God's grace and power, performed amazing miracles and signs among the people. But one day some men from the Synagogue of Freed Slaves, as it was called, started to debate with him. They were Jews from Cyrene, Alexandria, Cilicia, and the province of Asia. None of them could stand against the wisdom and the Spirit with which Stephen spoke.

So they persuaded some men to lie about Stephen, saying, "We heard him blaspheme Moses, and even God." This roused the people, the elders, and the teachers of religious law. So they arrested Stephen and brought him before the high council.

The lying witnesses said, "This man is always speaking against the holy Temple and against the law of Moses. We have heard him say that this Jesus of Nazareth will destroy the Temple and change the customs Moses handed down to us."

At this point everyone in the high council stared at Stephen, because his face became as bright as an angel's.

Why was Stephen experiencing suffering? How did he respond to the trials he was going through?

_____

_____

Read Acts 7:55.

Stephen, full of the Holy Spirit, gazed steadily into heaven and saw the glory of God, and he saw Jesus standing in the place of honor at God's right hand.

As Stephen is being dragged into the city to be stoned to death, what vision is revealed to him?

_____

_____

When Stephen was arrested and put on trial for his faith and given a chance to preach, the Holy Spirit overwhelmed him with a special revelation. God has prepared a special intimacy for those who suffer alongside him—a kind of intimacy that can only be experienced when we're facing trials and difficulties.

Read 1 Peter 4:14.

If you are insulted because you bear the name of Christ, you will be blessed, for the glorious Spirit of God rests upon you.

What does this verse say will happen for those who suffer because of Christ?

_____

_____

If we understand that suffering is an inevitable part of life, then our love for Christ will run deeper than the pain, grief, and sorrow we experience when we are stripped of our lesser comforts.

Why? Because all the things that we count on for our happiness, our stability, or our reward are nothing when compared with Jesus Christ.

> Everything else is worthless when compared with the infinite value of knowing Christ Jesus my Lord. For his sake I have discarded everything else, counting it all as garbage, so that I could gain Christ and become one with him. I no longer count on my own righteousness through obeying the law; rather, I become righteous through faith in Christ. For God's way of making us right with himself depends on faith. I want to know Christ and experience the mighty power that raised him from the dead. I want to suffer with him, sharing in his death, so that one way or another I will experience the resurrection from the dead!
>
> PHILIPPIANS 3:8-11

Suffering has a way of bringing us into the depths of knowing Jesus in a way we can never experience when our lives are "comfortable" and "happy." But this doesn't happen automatically. We have to be willing to dig deep and lean into him during those seasons of trials.

So what about you? Are you willing to go deep with Jesus?

Day 4

Faith anchors everything we do and everything we are as followers of Christ. It's the only way we can have a close, intimate relationship with him. I don't know about you, but I want to be close—*really* close. I mean, I want to be smell-his-breath-on-my-skin kind of close!

Before I experienced the deep end of faith, I knew the right answers. I knew, at least in my head, that faith was about trusting what I couldn't see. But it was just a cliché for me.

I don't want you to stay stuck like I was, so I'd like to invite you on an adventure with me. It's a journey of stepping out of a safe faith and embarking on a risk-taking faith.

From this point on, I hope you will toss aside shallow faith and your soul will shout, "Faith is so much more than that!"

In order to embrace a deeper level of faith, we need to understand what Scripture says is true about faith. Match the verse on the left to its corresponding truth on the right.

Romans 10:17	Faith is powerful enough to fight evil.
Galatians 5:6	We will only understand faith through hearing God's Word.
Hebrews 11:6	We are made right in God's sight through faith.
Ephesians 6:16	Faith isn't about ceremonies or rituals; it's expressed through love.
Romans 1:17	Without faith, we cannot please God.

Read Hebrews 13:12-14.

Jesus suffered and died outside the city gates to make his people holy by means of his own blood. So let us go out to him, outside the camp, and bear the disgrace he bore. For this world is not our permanent home; we are looking forward to a home yet to come.

What words or phrases stand out to you in this passage?

_____

_____

_____

This passage says that Jesus goes outside the camp or outside the gates. What do you think that means?

_____

_____

_____

In order for our minds to be blown when we read this passage, we need to think like the writer of Hebrews. He was most likely referencing the Israelites' mobile community that would settle for a time along a river or in a mountain valley. A camp was a place of safety for people. If you went outside the camp, you'd face dangers like wild animals, enemies, and the obvious threat of being vulnerable to the elements. The camp was a place of comfort, safety, and familiarity. In addition, according to Jewish tradition, the camp represented all that was sacred in their society, while everything outside the camp was considered unclean.

So when the author tells us to join Jesus "outside the camp," it's as if he is saying, "Hey, you—take a risk with me, be dangerous, step out of your comfort zone, be willing to get a little dirty."

When we step outside our "camp" of religious safety, we encounter people who don't look like us, talk like us, or act like us. Some places outside the camp are uncomfortable, muddy, and downright scary. But there are lost and needy men and women and children who are living in darkness and in need of the light we can bring from the warm, safe huddle of our camp.

Who in your life is "outside the camp"? What would it look like to bring light to them?

_____

_____

_____

Journal about a time you took a risk for God. What was the experience like? How did you feel before you went for it? How did you feel when it was all over?

_____

_____

_____

Journal about a time you felt God asking you to take a risk and you chose not to do it. What regrets did you have afterward?

_____

_____

_____

What holds you back from taking risks for God?

_____

_____

_____

Do you want this life-changing, gut-wrenching, as-close-as-your-breath faith? If so, you have to be willing to go outside the camp.

Day 5

For most of us, death and danger are most likely not at the top of our bucket lists. But if we dig into Scripture, we realize that perhaps they should be.

At the very least, the Bible makes it clear that we'd be wise to ponder our own death. That may sound morbid or senseless, but when we do so in a healthy way, it's actually a faith-building experience.

> You sweep people away like dreams that disappear.
>   They are like grass that springs up in the morning.
> In the morning it blooms and flourishes,
>   but by evening it is dry and withered.
> We wither beneath your anger;
>   we are overwhelmed by your fury.
> You spread out our sins before you—
>   our secret sins—and you see them all.
> We live our lives beneath your wrath,
>   ending our years with a groan.
>
> Seventy years are given to us!
>   Some even live to eighty.
> But even the best years are filled with pain and trouble;
>   soon they disappear, and we fly away.
> Who can comprehend the power of your anger?
>   Your wrath is as awesome as the fear you deserve.

Teach us to realize the brevity of life,
  so that we may grow in wisdom.
PSALM 90:5-12

What does this psalm say we can expect about life on this earth?

_____

_____

How does a healthy perspective on the brevity of life affect our faith?

_____

_____

Before I received my cancer diagnosis, I suppose this psalm would have seemed sad to me. But now I breathe it in like life-giving medicine—especially that last part about pondering our own mortality so we can grow in wisdom. Now I know what the psalmist meant when he talked about "the brevity of life."

I didn't know how much I needed God when everything was going fine in my life. It was only when things fell apart that I realized how desperate I was for him—even in the things I thought I was in control of. I didn't need God until it was time for me to number my days.

List some areas of your life that seem easy, manageable, and comfortable—circumstances in which you rarely think to consider God.

_____

_____

Numbering our days doesn't have to be a scary thing. It just means remembering that our lives are short and that we need to spend our days with an eternal perspective. Great wisdom—life-revolutionizing wisdom—comes from periodically pondering these things.

If we run away from the truth that we are simply a mist that appears for a moment and then vanishes, we become arrogant and fail to recognize how much we need God. We begin to believe that we are the masters of our lives and forget that we owe every moment to the sovereign will of God. But if we look our suffering and impending death in the face, then we will have the humility to yield ourselves to God.

Take a moment to number your days before the Lord. How do you feel about suffering—whether in the present or in the future? How do you feel when you think about the brevity of life?

_____

_____

Read Philippians 1:29.

For you have been given not only the privilege of trusting in Christ but also the privilege of suffering for him.

This passage makes the surprising statement that it's not only a privilege to trust Christ but also a privilege to do what? How does this change your perspective on suffering?

_____

_____

Read Hebrews 2:18.

Since he himself has gone through suffering and testing, he is able to help us when we are being tested.

What does it mean to you that Jesus went through suffering and testing himself?

_____

_____

Read James 5:11.

We give great honor to those who endure under suffering. For instance, you know about Job, a man of great endurance. You can see how the Lord was kind to him at the end, for the Lord is full of tenderness and mercy.

What does the story of Job show us about God's character and how he treats us in the long term?

_____

_____

The question isn't whether we'll face suffering in our lives; it's how we will respond when we do. Will suffering break our faith or make it stronger?

Questions for Group Discussion or Personal Reflection

1. In your own words, how would you define faith? What role does it play in your relationship with God?

_____

_____

2. Looking back over the course of your life, how has your faith changed and grown?

_____

_____

3. What questions do you have about faith?

_____

_____

4. Which of God's characteristics do you most often relate to (Father, Friend, Helper, Redeemer, Shepherd, Lord, Fighter, etc.)?

_____

_____

5. Have you ever considered God as someone who would pick a fight with you? How does it make you feel to think of him in this way?

_____

_____

6. How do you respond when bad things happen to you? Do you get angry and blame God? Do you ask him for guidance and encouragement? What do you think your responses reveal about your faith?

_____

_____

7. Think of a time when you remained close to God in your suffering and a time when you did not. What do you think accounted for the difference?

_____

_____

8. On day 4 we discussed going "outside the camp." What is your huddle—the place where you feel safe and comfortable? What would it look like to take a risk and go outside your camp for the sake of Christ?

_____

_____

9. Have you ever taken the time to ponder your death? How do you think your life would be different if you had an increased awareness of the brevity of life?

_____

_____

10. What Scripture verse mentioned in the study so far do you want to cling to this week as you consider what deep, authentic faith looks like?

_____

_____

Week 2
·············
What Do You Really Believe?

Remember the things I have done in the past.
    For I alone am God!
    I am God, and there is none like me.
Only I can tell you the future
    before it even happens.
Everything I plan will come to pass,
    for I do whatever I wish.

ISAIAH 46:9-10

God is not a fortune-teller or someone who makes guesses about the future or a force that operates based on the luck of the draw. He doesn't need a crystal ball. He knows what's coming because he has planned it to come.

God has the rightful authority, freedom, wisdom, and power to accomplish *whatever* he wills, *whenever* he wills, and *however* he wills. In other words, God is sovereign. He plans and governs the movement and direction of all things while simultaneously existing *in* all things.

Isaiah 46 records these words from God: "Everything I plan will come to pass." In other words, nothing happens in the universe except for what he wants to happen.

In order for us to track further into the deep woods of faith, we must come face-to-face with the truth of God's sovereignty.

As we go through this study, I encourage you to wrestle with the "unmentionables" of Christianity—the topics, ideas, and conversations that aren't comfortable or safe to discuss in most religious settings. The sovereignty of God is one of those scary truths that leave no human unchanged, and therefore it's rarely pondered or spoken about out loud.

It's one thing to think about God's sovereignty—that alone would be enough to keep a person speechless and drooling for days. But for us to remain faithful to God's sovereignty—well, that means surrendering to having our minds permanently blown.

Before one can understand faith, one must understand God's sovereignty. Not to its fullest, of course—that's impossible on this side of glory. But we as humans need to recognize that there is no other hope for humanity outside of a God who does what he wants, when he wants.

We may claim to believe that God is sovereign, but that conviction is tested when tragedy strikes. When we're holding the hand of someone who has just lost her child or spouse or parent and her weeping eyes look into ours, how do we respond? When a terrorist detonates a bomb that kills hundreds of civilians or a tornado rips through a nearby town or children go hungry, what do we believe to be true of God? The words that come out of our mouths often stand contrary to the truth that God is, in fact, sovereign.

The reality is, we don't know what to say. On the inside we're screaming, *How could you, God?* As much as we love God and believe in him, we can't make heads or tails of the tragedy. Why would a loving God allow such suffering in the world? How could a merciful God let this happen? Why do good people suffer while the evil prosper?

And so we echo the words that we've heard during another tragedy—words spoken by a preacher, a friend, a radio host, or a professor. It sounded good then, so we parrot it back now. It goes something like this: "Well, suffering is just a part of this sinful world we live in. We know that nothing evil or bad comes from God, but he does allow us to go through bad or difficult times in order to make us stronger, more faithful people."

Sound familiar?

It certainly does to me. I've used it plenty of times myself. But lately I've been wrestling with that word *allow*. Try using it in other sentences, like, "Oh sure, I would *allow* my child to do that" or "*Allow* me" or "I will not *allow* that to happen in my house!"

To me, the word *allow* gives the idea that there is another alternative, another option besides the one being allowed.

If the Bible is true, and therefore the passage from Isaiah is true, then it certainly sounds like God is not simply "allowing" things to happen. He is arranging them, planning them, scheduling them out on his heavenly itinerary. He is not only sovereign over all the righteous things that happen but sovereign over all the evil as well.

I don't know about you, but God just picked a fight with me . . . a fight over what I *really* believe.

Welcome to week 2.

Day 1

To start our study today, I'd like to open with a brief story that happened a couple of thousand years ago but could just as easily have taken place today.

"He's coming! He's coming! He's outside the village now!"

As the words rang out through the grief-stricken shadows of her home, Martha let the small cup she'd been relentlessly scrubbing come crashing to the floor. Her brow was covered in beads of sweat, and she gasped as the tears threatened to spill over.

She'd known somewhere deep inside that he would come, but that confidence had been strangled bit by bit with each day that had passed since her brother's death. Yet even her deep grief and disappointment were no match for the small flame of hope that flickered to life when she heard he was near.

Martha's emotions were playing tricks on her, it seemed. Simply hearing that Jesus was on his way reignited her hope—the same hope she'd felt the day she sent word for him to come right away. But now it was four days later, and Lazarus's lifeless body remained untouched by the miracle of healing she'd been hoping for.

She had prayed desperately that Jesus would come in time, but God hadn't answered her prayers. Day and night, weeping and wailing beside her brother's lifeless body, she'd pleaded for God's mercy, yet he hadn't come to Lazarus's aid.

As she stood beside her washbasin, her mind told her to stay, to finish cleaning the dishes and forget about Jesus. After all, hadn't he forgotten about her?

And yet her heart tugged her extremities into motion, pulling her body toward the only one who had the power over life and death.

When her eyes met Jesus on the rocky path outside her home, all she thought she knew crumbled as she fell to the ground. She could not contain her grief and love as she collapsed at Jesus' feet. "Lord, if only you had been here, my brother would not have died."

As her body trembled before him, she felt a sudden wave of peace and warmth overwhelm her as Jesus placed his hand gently on top of her head. As she looked up at him, she gasped at what she saw—tears! Tangible traces of sadness had broken through the dust and grime on her Savior's face.

And as she watched her Lord weep, she loved him more, trusted him more, and believed him more—despite the pain that told her to do otherwise.

Read John 10:31-33, 39-42.

The people picked up stones to kill him. Jesus said, "At my Father's direction I have done many good works. For which one are you going to stone me?"

They replied, "We're stoning you not for any good work, but for blasphemy! You, a mere man, claim to be God." . . .

Once again they tried to arrest him, but he got away and left them. He went beyond the Jordan River near the place where John was first baptizing and stayed there awhile. And many followed him. "John didn't perform miraculous signs," they remarked to one another, "but everything he said about this man has come true." And many who were there believed in Jesus.

Twice in this passage the crowds harassed Jesus. What did they attempt to do to him?

_____

_____

_____

_____

After Jesus escaped, where did he go? How long did he stay there?

Now read John 11:1-3.

A man named Lazarus was sick. He lived in Bethany with his sisters, Mary and Martha. This is the Mary who later poured the expensive perfume on the Lord's feet and wiped them with her hair. Her brother, Lazarus, was sick. So the two sisters sent a message to Jesus telling him, "Lord, your dear friend is very sick."

Where was Lazarus from?

_____

_____

When Jesus received word that his friend Lazarus was sick, he and his disciples were about twenty miles from Bethany, where Lazarus lay dying. If the messenger who brought word to him had traveled quickly, he could have made the trip to Jesus in one day's time.

Based on verse 3, what was Lazarus's relationship to Jesus?

_____

_____

_____

_____

It would only seem right and loving for the Lord to stop what he was doing and hightail it to Lazarus's house upon hearing of his friend's terminal illness. I mean, he was only one day's travel away. And yet . . .

Read John 11:4-7.

When Jesus heard about it he said, "Lazarus's sickness will not end in death. No, it happened for the glory of God so that the Son of God will receive glory from this." So although Jesus loved Martha, Mary, and Lazarus, he stayed where he was for the next two days. Finally, he said to his disciples, "Let's go back to Judea."

Based on this passage, how many days did Jesus wait before he left for Bethany?

_____

The Bible makes it clear that there was a strong friendship between Jesus and Lazarus, yet Jesus' actions seem to contradict this truth. And perhaps even more hard hitting is the fact that Jesus, being God in flesh, already knew that Lazarus was sick before the messenger told him, and he also knew that Lazarus would die from the sickness before Jesus made it there. In short, Jesus loved Lazarus—and he let Lazarus die.

The worst-case scenario happened: Lazarus died, and before that he most likely suffered greatly (without the benefit of the pain management we have today). His sisters most likely stood by, helplessly watching his torment drag on until he breathed his last. They wrapped his body and buried him, all the while wondering, *Where is Jesus? Why didn't he come?*

This was real death. Real loss. And Jesus didn't show up to stop it.

Think of a time in your life when your circumstance seemed to contradict a God of love. Journal the emotions you felt at that time.

_____

_____

_____

What request have you brought before God that he has yet to answer?

_____

_____

_____

When God delays in coming to our aid when we most desperately need him, what effect does it have on our faith?

_____

_____

_____

There's nothing easy about choosing to believe God is completely in control. There's nothing easy about believing God is sovereign over everything that happens in our lives—including seasons of great pain, illness, suffering, and even death.

It wasn't easy for the disciples, who waited alongside a grieving Jesus for two days while his friend lay dying only a day's walk away. It wasn't easy for the sisters, who believed Jesus would heal their brother before it was too late, only to be proven wrong.

And it wasn't easy for Jesus, who was human enough to feel sorrow and grief over his dear friend, just like we do.

But as we will see in day 2, there is a reason for every move God makes. And it is this reason alone that has the power to keep our hearts faithful even when our minds are not.

Day 2

I'm no doctor, but I believe there is a supernatural moment that occurs within the twenty-four to forty-eight hours prior to a person's death. I don't have scientific degrees to back this up—just my experiences from witnessing fifty-plus deaths during my time with hospice, an end-of-life care organization. But the three most significant deaths I had a front-row seat to were those of my stepfather, my mother, and my grandfather.

With each of these family members, I stood back in shock, awe, grief, joy, and pain—a mixture of almost every emotion—and watched this supernatural moment play out before my eyes.

Some people experience a surge of normalcy prior to death, which is sometimes referred to as an awakening. Doctors believe that as the brain loses oxygen and as blood pressure decreases, neurons begin to fire at a rapid rate, causing a sudden surge of brain waves just before death.

When this happened to my stepfather, he sat up, spoke about heaven, and formed complete sentences about going home. At the end of my mom's life, she came out of a comatose state and sat up and smiled at each of her children as we said good-bye, despite a previous stroke that had impaired her speech. And I will never forget how appropriate Papa's awakening was. He sat straight up in bed with his two collapsed lungs and looked straight at me.

"Papa, do you know who I am?" I asked.

In his sassy way, he responded, "Well of course I do, Kasey! Now get me some ice cream!"

We laughed with him as he ate his final scoop of vanilla ice cream (in this life anyway).

I share these personal stories with you because I think there's a spiritual parallel to this idea. I'd like you to think back to your own moments of awakening that have occurred just when you thought you were at the end—moments when your pain and sorrow were deepest, moments that seemed to contradict the practical reality of the situation.

Even when it seems like it's too late for a miracle, when God has waited too long to show up, when we're past the point of all hope, we can still have one anchor for our hearts.

God's love.

Read John 11:4-7 again.

When Jesus heard about it he said, "Lazarus's sickness will not end in death. No, it happened for the glory of God so that the Son of God will receive glory from this." So although Jesus loved Martha, Mary, and Lazarus, he stayed where he was for the next two days. Finally, he said to his disciples, "Let's go back to Judea."

How did Jesus feel toward Lazarus and his sisters?

_____

_____

Did you catch that? "So although Jesus loved Martha, Mary, and Lazarus, he stayed where he was for the next two days." *So*—a small but important word to understanding this breathtaking truth. Jesus loved Mary and Martha, *so* he traveled to Bethany.

From what we learned in day 1, why was Bethany a dangerous place for Jesus to return to? (Note: Bethany was only two miles from Jerusalem.)

_____

_____

What could possibly motivate Jesus to reenter a place where people wanted to kill him? You've got it—love.

But here's the "awakening" part. Here's where what we know doesn't seem to match what we see. Where those last moments, although precious and appreciated, can be painful at the same time.

We see that Jesus' motivation was love. We read that he was willing to risk his life to go to Bethany. But we also must wrestle with the fact that it was this same love that let Lazarus die. It was this love that let my stepfather, my mother, and my grandfather die as well.

Love lets people die. Love lets people get hurt and suffer. Love lets people experience disappointment and unanswered prayers.

When is it hardest for you to experience God's love?

_____

_____

Describe a few times you've felt God's love most tangibly.

_____

_____

_____

_____

God's love is the inspiration and motivation for every move he makes—even the ones we don't understand. When our faith is rocked by a devastating blow to what we think we know about God, ourselves, or others, the hard truth is this: love is always and every time the instigator.

Day 3

I'm thankful for the disciples' role in Scripture, because they always make me feel just a little bit better about my own human reactions to Jesus. On many occasions during their time with Jesus, the disciples were left drooling and scratching their heads. "Uh . . . what?"

At times they answered his questions all wrong, and other times they completely doubted him. Sometimes they were downright stupid!

But hey, I get it. They're a lot like me.

Let's take a look at how they responded in the story of Lazarus.

Read John 11:8-15.

His disciples objected. "Rabbi," they said, "only a few days ago the people in Judea were trying to stone you. Are you going there again?"

Jesus replied, "There are twelve hours of daylight every day. During the day people can walk safely. They can see because they have the light of this world. But at night there is danger of stumbling because they have no light." Then he said, "Our friend Lazarus has fallen asleep, but now I will go and wake him up."

The disciples said, "Lord, if he is sleeping, he will soon get better!" They thought Jesus meant Lazarus was simply sleeping, but Jesus meant Lazarus had died.

So he told them plainly, "Lazarus is dead. And for your sakes, I'm glad I wasn't there, for now you will really believe. Come, let's go see him."

I don't know about you, but I read this passage and think, *Hey, brothers, I hear ya!*

Call me the dunce in the corner of the classroom, but Jesus said Lazarus was asleep, so just wake him up, right?

Then we read, "He told them *plainly*." Yep—that confirms my hypothesis. We're pretty stupid—I mean "plain," as Jesus put it.

Think of specific times in your life when Jesus seemed to be speaking clearly to you but you misunderstood what he was saying. For example, you know he was saying "Go!" but you went in the wrong direction, or you felt a clear freedom to date a certain person but you picked the wrong guy.

_____

_____

The truth is, you and I will show our humanity (or "plainness") most of the time. We are often well intentioned enough—we desire to hear God speaking to us, but we're in a rush for the answer or we think we know the answer before he gives it. This was the case for the disciples. When Jesus told them Lazarus was asleep, they responded with a human response: "Lord, if he is sleeping, he will soon get better!"

Their answer was common, easy, and probable.

Yet God is none of these things.

Write the ways God shows his love to us, according to the following verses:

My old self has been crucified with Christ. It is no longer I who live, but Christ lives in me. So I live in this earthly body by trusting in the Son of God, who loved me and gave himself for me.

GALATIANS 2:20

_____

_____

Christ's love controls us. Since we believe that Christ died for all, we also believe that we have all died to our old life.

2 CORINTHIANS 5:14

_____

_____

God showed his great love for us by sending Christ to die for us while we were still sinners.
ROMANS 5:8

_____

_____

Can anything ever separate us from Christ's love? Does it mean he no longer loves us if we have trouble or calamity, or are persecuted, or hungry, or destitute, or in danger, or threatened with death? (As the Scriptures say, "For your sake we are killed every day; we are being slaughtered like sheep.") No, despite all these things, overwhelming victory is ours through Christ, who loved us.

And I am convinced that nothing can ever separate us from God's love. Neither death nor life, neither angels nor demons, neither our fears for today nor our worries about tomorrow—not even the powers of hell can separate us from God's love. No power in the sky above or in the earth below—indeed, nothing in all creation will ever be able to separate us from the love of God that is revealed in Christ Jesus our Lord.
ROMANS 8:35-39

_____

_____

Before the Passover celebration, Jesus knew that his hour had come to leave this world and return to his Father. He had loved his disciples during his ministry on earth, and now he loved them to the very end.
JOHN 13:1

_____

_____

And this is merely scratching the surface of God's love for us; we will never reach its depths on this side of glory. But his love looked different than the disciples imagined—and it's different from what we expect too.

Jesus let Lazarus die. Plain and simple. He could have gone to Bethany earlier, healed Lazarus before he died, and had a party to celebrate afterward. But no, Jesus lingered. In his love, he lingered. And rather than look at the hard truth about their Lord, the disciples looked for the easy answer. Just as we often do.

The hard truth is this: sometimes the love of Jesus lingers.

We cry out to God, but he doesn't answer.

We long for relief or release, but it doesn't come.

We run so fast and so hard, but we never reach the finish line.

We get tired of waiting, so we step out on our own terms.

We think we know the answer God will give us, so we test it out prematurely.

When God's love lingers, we get antsy. And this is the point of our faith where the real believers stand up while the phonies give up.

Jesus knew he would wait two days until Lazarus was not just a little bit dead but a lot dead. But it was not God in the flesh who needed a lesson in faith and love. Jesus chose his actions wisely, for they would impact many people—the disciples, Martha and Mary, the extended family grieving alongside them, and the whole community.

Jesus didn't need to know where these people stood in their faith—they needed to know where they stood themselves. And so they were about to get a serious lesson in believing God over their circumstances. Or as I like to say, Jesus just picked a fight with their faith.

Look at this list of possible reactions to tests of faith. Circle the ways you have responded in the past when God has lingered in his love in order to show you your faith.

In the past when God has lingered, I have . . .

picked up an addiction or gone back to an old one

become angry

gotten bitter

wished for death

become depressed

gotten discouraged

let my marriage or other significant relationships fall apart

become violent toward myself or others

become jealous of those God seemed to be blessing

become overwhelmed with fear and anxiety

clung to unforgiveness

allowed guilt and shame to get the best of me

basked in my loneliness and despair
blamed God or others in the wait
allowed stress to take over all the time
become a workaholic
stopped waiting and started doing my own thing
lost all hope in God
other:

As difficult as it is to see in the midst of the lingering, everything God does is motivated by love. He often allows his love to linger in order to show us that his love for us is anything but common—just as he did for Martha.

God sees the full potential for our lives, and he deeply desires an intimate relationship with us. God never lingers out of wrath or anger, but out of a pure and holy desire for us to believe he's bigger than we did prior to our season of waiting.

Jesus longed for his disciples to be used in a supernatural way, so he pulled out some supernatural lessons to prepare them for greatness. He's ready to do the same for us.

As we wrap up today's lesson, I encourage you to journal your answers to the following questions and meditate on God's love as you do.

How are you making less of God's love for you right now? In what ways are you trying to make it common, rational, and reasonable instead of allowing it to be something more unexplainable and supernatural?

_____

_____

Are you currently experiencing the lingering of God's love? In what ways?

_____

_____

Write down some ways you can begin to trust God more during this waiting time. Are there unhealthy behaviors you can replace with healthy ones? Is there an accountability group or prayer partner you could meet with? What spiritual disciplines (such as memorizing Scripture) could you be intentional about to help give you peace as you wait?

_____

_____

Day 4

Let's continue with Lazarus's story through Martha's eyes.

> When Jesus arrived at Bethany, he was told that Lazarus had already been in his grave for four days. Bethany was only a few miles down the road from Jerusalem, and many of the people had come to console Martha and Mary in their loss. When Martha got word that Jesus was coming, she went to meet him. But Mary stayed in the house. Martha said to Jesus, "Lord, if only you had been here, my brother would not have died. But even now I know that God will give you whatever you ask."
>
> Jesus told her, "Your brother will rise again."
>
> JOHN 11:17-23

As Martha wept, I picture Jesus gently lifting her face to meet his and then, with loving intensity, speaking over her, "Your brother will rise again."

As his living words began to revive her hope, she might have wondered, *Could he mean . . . ? No, surely not.* She dared not let herself hope in that way. Not after four days.

"He will rise when everyone else rises, at the last day," she finally said (verse 24).

And her statement was true. Lazarus would rise again on the last day. In fact, Martha most likely had no idea how deeply Jesus longed for that day. But Jesus was referring to something more in that moment.

He replied, "I am the resurrection and the life. Anyone who believes in me will live, even after dying. Everyone who lives in me and believes in me will never ever die. Do you believe this?" (verses 25-26).

The power of Jesus' words must have caused faith to swell in Martha's soul—an awakening, one might say.

I doubt she was sure what it all meant, but as Jesus spoke, it was as if death itself was being swallowed up (see 1 Corinthians 15:54). No one else had ever spoken like this man (see John 7:46).

Martha answered, "I have always believed you are the Messiah, the Son of God, the one who has come into the world from God" (verse 27).

Like Martha, have you ever believed in God even when your mind or your circumstances were telling you not to? Has there ever been a time when your soul was on fire for the truth of God despite the pain around you? Describe that experience below.

_____

_____

_____

You know how this story ends, right?

Lazarus *does* wake up.

But in the horrible days before that, during Lazarus's agonizing illness and in the dark misery of the days after his death, Martha didn't know what God was doing. He seemed silent and unresponsive. Jesus didn't come. She was confused, disappointed, and overwhelmed with grief.

Yet Jesus delayed precisely because he loved Martha and Mary and Lazarus. He knew that Lazarus's death and resurrection would give maximum glory to God and that his friends would experience maximum joy in that glory.

Read 2 Corinthians 4:17.

Our present troubles are small and won't last very long. Yet they produce for us a glory that vastly outweighs them and will last forever!

What does this verse mean to you? Put it in your own words.

_____

_____

When Jesus makes a trusting saint wait in pain, his reasons are only and always love. God ordains his child's deep disappointment and profound suffering in order to give him or her far greater joy in the glory he is preparing to reveal.

Read Romans 8:18.

What we suffer now is nothing compared to the glory he will reveal to us later.

How have you seen this verse to be true in your life or in the lives of people you know?

_____

_____

Before we know what Jesus is doing, circumstances can look all wrong, and we're tempted to interpret God's apparent inaction as a lack of love, when in fact God is showing us love in the most profound way.

The question for us is the same as it was for Martha when Jesus peered into her eyes and asked, "Do you believe this?"

Day 5

God chose to pick a fight with Martha's belief system, pushing her into a place of wrestling with what she really believed—not for God's sake, but for hers. She had to choose whether she'd trust her circumstances or the lingering love of Jesus.

Because faith expresses itself through love (see Galatians 5:6), love is the anchor of the purest, most raw form of faith.

So what is love?

True love is when we're given what we need most.

And what we need most is not healing or answers or smooth circumstances.

What we need most in this life is a full and endless experience of the glory of God. And that is exactly what Martha got.

> Jesus responded, "Didn't I tell you that you would see God's glory if you believe?" So they rolled the stone aside. Then Jesus looked up to heaven and said, "Father, thank you for hearing me. You always hear me, but I said it out loud for the sake of all these people standing here, so that they will believe you sent me." Then Jesus shouted, "Lazarus, come out!" And the dead man came out, his hands and feet bound in graveclothes, his face wrapped in a headcloth. Jesus told them, "Unwrap him and let him go!"
>
> JOHN 11:40-44

This is what it's like to be loved by Jesus.

It is not a feeling of temporary happiness or success or thrill. Love is when God allows us into his glory.

Love is when God gives us a moment to admire and marvel and bask in his mighty power to work in all things—even through us as sinners.

Love is when God acts out of sovereignty, in control over the good and the bad, even when we don't understand it.

So Jesus planned Lazarus's death in order to show the glory of God and to intensify the faith of his disciples and all others touched by this event.

Raw faith is being satisfied in the glory of Christ alone as he loves us and awakens in us a faith that doesn't waver with suffering or circumstances.

In those days between the death of Lazarus and his resurrection four days later, his family and friends couldn't see how God would be glorified in it. If that's where you stand today, don't make a judgment before the resurrection. God is doing more than you can know. And the resurrection will bring all of it to light. In the meantime, trust him and treasure him above all things.

List some areas in your life where you are currently aware of God's glory.

_____

_____

Now list some areas in your life where you are struggling to see God's glory.

_____

_____

I strongly encourage you to memorize the following verses as a way to seal week 2 of our study.

Christ is the visible image of the invisible God.
    He existed before anything was created and is supreme over all creation,
for through him God created everything
    in the heavenly realms and on earth.
He made the things we can see
    and the things we can't see—
such as thrones, kingdoms, rulers, and authorities in the unseen world.
    Everything was created through him and for him.
He existed before anything else,
    and he holds all creation together.
COLOSSIANS 1:15-17

Nothing in this universe exists for its own sake. Everything, from the sunrise each morning to the final breath of our loved ones, exists to make Christ's glory more fully known.

I don't know about you, but I don't want to serve a God who simply sits by and allows things to happen on this earth. I desire to worship an all-knowing, all-powerful, all-sovereign God who controls everything. Even the things I don't understand.

Questions for Group Discussion or Personal Reflection

1. Read Isaiah 46:9-10. What do you think it means that God is sovereign over the past and the future? What does this mean for your own life?

_____

_____

_____

_____

2. God says, "Everything I plan will come to pass, for I do whatever I wish" (Isaiah 46:10). How does it make you feel to read that God's plans will take place, no matter what? Does this truth move you toward feelings of confusion or clarity?

_____

_____

_____

_____

3. What are some ways you have seen God's sovereignty in dealing with this world?

_____

_____

_____

_____

4. In what ways have you seen God's sovereignty in your own life?

_____

_____

_____

_____

5. When do you tend to doubt God's sovereignty?

_____

_____

_____

_____

6. How would you answer this question: Why do bad things happen to good
people?

_____

_____

_____

_____

7. How important do you think our beliefs are to growing deeper in faith with God?

_____

_____

_____

_____

8. What are some ways you feel that God has "picked a fight" with your belief
system or the things you've always assumed to be true?

_____

_____

_____

_____

9. Give some examples of times God's love has lingered in your life—times when
you desperately needed him yet his love seemed far away.

_____

_____

_____

_____

10. Looking back, can you see why God lingered the way he did? Did you grow more faithful in the wait, or did you become bitter?

_____

_____

_____

_____

Week 3

Frustrated with Faith

When we experience frustration with faith and our doubts drag us down, leaving us exhausted and beaten, there's a critical truth we need to cling to about the God who loves us: he is not shocked by our doubts or left to despair. God isn't surprised or bewildered by our struggles with faith. He isn't sitting behind a desk, scratching his head and typing out a list of pros and cons about whether to keep us around or wipe us out with a lightning bolt.

In fact, God knew we'd wrestle with doubts about him long before he said, "Let there be light." God is so in tune with our humanness and our tendency to question him that he was sure to include plenty of examples in Scripture of other people who wrestled over this. And this week I'd like to devote some time to unpacking the story of one of those individuals.

We'll draw from one man's questions about God—a man who gets only a few pages of Scripture and doesn't have many little boys named after him. In fact, I didn't even know this guy had his own book in the Bible until a few years ago, when one of my seminary professors drew my attention to it.

Although this man was a prophet by calling and his book is in the genre of prophecy in the Bible, his ministry reads more like a journal entry than a proclamation. His writing is intensely personal and practical, and it grants us a clear understanding of God's relationship with those who wrestle to believe him.

Our companion and fellow journeyer for the week ahead is a man named Habakkuk.

Day 1

Let's begin by reading Habakkuk 1:1-4.

This is the message that the prophet Habakkuk received in a vision.

How long, O Lord, must I call for help?
    But you do not listen!
"Violence is everywhere!" I cry,
    but you do not come to save.
Must I forever see these evil deeds?
    Why must I watch all this misery?
Wherever I look,
    I see destruction and violence.
I am surrounded by people
    who love to argue and fight.
The law has become paralyzed,
    and there is no justice in the courts.
The wicked far outnumber the righteous,
    so that justice has become perverted.

Based on these first few verses, how would you describe Habakkuk's tone? (Check all that apply.)

☐ upbeat
☐ timid

☐ depressed
☐ whiny
☐ positive
☐ doubtful

Habakkuk starts out talking to God in a way that most of us are quite familiar with—whining. He's basically complaining to God that he doesn't like the way things are going in his nation and he wants God to do something about it.

Can you relate? I know I can.

Write about a time when you flat-out didn't like what God seemed to be doing. What did you communicate to him during this time? What was your tone like?

_____

_____

_____

Read the following passage, looking for God's response to Habakkuk:

The LORD replied,

"Look around at the nations;
    look and be amazed!
For I am doing something in your own day,
    something you wouldn't believe
    even if someone told you about it.
I am raising up the Babylonians,
    a cruel and violent people.
They will march across the world
    and conquer other lands.
They are notorious for their cruelty
    and do whatever they like.
Their horses are swifter than cheetahs
    and fiercer than wolves at dusk.
Their charioteers charge from far away.
    Like eagles, they swoop down to devour their prey.

"On they come, all bent on violence.
    Their hordes advance like a desert wind,
    sweeping captives ahead of them like sand.
They scoff at kings and princes
    and scorn all their fortresses.
They simply pile ramps of earth
    against their walls and capture them!
They sweep past like the wind
    and are gone.
But they are deeply guilty,
    for their own strength is their god."

HABAKKUK 1:5-11

How did God respond to Habakkuk's whining?

☐ God seems to beat around the bush, not giving Habakkuk a clear response.
☐ God tells Habakkuk he is being a whiny baby and he doesn't appreciate the way Habakkuk is speaking to him.
☐ God says, *Look, dude, I have a plan. I'll even tell you some of it, but you are still not going to get it. You're just going to have to trust me.*

The majority of the book of Habakkuk pretty much repeats the following exchange:

Habakkuk: What are you doing?

God: Look. I know what I'm doing.

Habakkuk: Are you sure you know what you're doing?

God: I'm sure I know what I'm doing.

Habakkuk: Hey, do you *really* know what you're doing?

God: Yeah, I *really* know what I'm doing! I'm God, remember?

Habakkuk: Oh, wow, you do know what you're doing!

That's the book of Habakkuk in a nutshell—a series of conversations between a man and the God he believes in—sort of. Over and over we see this guy asking God what the plan is. And over and over we find ourselves doing the same thing Habakkuk did—asking God, "Hey, what's the plan?"

We want to know the big picture of what God is doing. We want to see the final scene. And yet the answer God gave Habakkuk is the same response he gives us time and time again: *Even if I told you, Child, you still wouldn't understand.*

Like Habakkuk, we must learn to trust God—even when we don't like what he's doing, even when we don't understand what he's up to, even when we struggle with our own doubts.

When Habakkuk asks God these recurring questions, it's clear that he isn't just looking for information; he's looking for truth.

Read the following verses, looking for how the Bible defines truth:

Jesus told him, "I am the way, the truth, and the life. No one can come to the Father except through me.
JOHN 14:6

All who love the truth recognize that what I say is true.
JOHN 18:37

The truth lives in us and will be with us forever.
2 JOHN 1:2

What theme runs through these verses?

_____

_____

_____

_____

If we want to experience real faith, we must be desperate for the truth; we need the truth to know real faith. We hear so many conflicting messages in our world. Some people say, "Well, there are many gods" or "There's no God" or "There's no life after death" or "Everybody goes to heaven" or "Good people go to heaven." There are all sorts of different opinions, conjectures, and speculations in our world. But what is the real truth?

Read John 14:6 again and then write it in the space below.

_____

_____

_____

_____

Jesus didn't just say that he'd show us the truth; he said he *is* the truth. That means that if we really want to grasp truth, we can't just believe it in our heads; we have to take it a step further and make it *our* truth. We must accept it—not fight it, deny it, resist it, or whine about it, but receive it. If our faith doesn't reach down and connect with everyday life, our perceived rights, our relationships, what we eat, how we spend our money, how we talk, and all the other details of our day-to-day lives, then we are not walking in truth.

Information in and of itself cannot save us or place us in right relationship with God. Many people are equipped with loads of information, but until it is practiced as faith, they lack transformation. Every time we pick up our Bibles, we find ourselves in the same position as Habakkuk—asking questions of God, not just to find information, but to seek truth. God has come to reveal himself to us; he has come to tell us the truth. And in return, he wants us to hear, believe, and obey what he's saying—regardless of whether we agree with it or whether we can see it.

Day 2

As we get into the book of Habakkuk, we recognize that the problem Habakkuk was facing is the same problem we have today. It's the same problem we humans have had ever since Genesis 3, and that's sin.

Sin causes all of humanity's problems. It comes in a variety of forms—rebellion, folly, suffering, injustice, death, wickedness, or evil. Sometimes it can result in depression, discouragement, or despair. Simply put, all the things we hate about our world come out of the belly of sin.

It is sin that permeates our world, and it is sin that plagues us—as people, as cultures, and as societies—from generation to generation. We live in a world where people experience pain and injustice. We go through suffering ourselves, and we cause others to suffer too—mentally, physically, spiritually, emotionally. We often die in pain, yet pain and suffering are some of the most consistent indicators that we're alive.

Things were no different for Habakkuk. When he looked around, he saw that sin was causing pain and suffering and injustice for his people. And he had a lot of questions about that.

As God's image bearers, we have the rare privilege of being able to think about the condition of our world. Other creatures, like animals, do not. They simply live out the existence they've been given—they don't speculate about the condition of their lives. We, however, have philosophy and therapy and religion and spirituality. And we have big questions, like *Why does the world look like this? Why is this happening to me? Why do people have to suffer? Why is there evil and injustice? Why am I experiencing pain? Why must we die? Why are things the way they are instead of the way we think they should be?*

Habakkuk struggled with those same questions. Specifically, he struggled with trusting God. And the beautiful truth we learn through his story is this: God is okay with our questions.

What questions do you have (or have you had in the past) for God? Write down your top three questions for him.

Question #1:

_____

_____

Question #2:

_____

_____

Question #3:

_____

_____

It isn't a sin to come to God and say, "I know you are good, and I know you are faithful, but I don't understand. This doesn't make any sense. People who don't take care of their bodies are healthy, and here I'm sick. People who don't want children have them, but my husband and I, who desperately want a child, can't have one. People who don't work hard have jobs, while I've busted my tail all my life only to find myself unemployed. I don't understand, God. It doesn't seem like there's any justice in my life. I don't understand."

It's okay to go to God with those inquiries and questions. It is not, however, okay to blame God. That's a reversal of the relationship. We can follow Habakkuk's example in this: he managed to question without blaming.

What is Habakkuk's first question for God?

How long, O LORD, must I call for help?
    But you do not listen!
HABAKKUK 1:2

_____

_____

Many of us have asked God a similar question: "God, why didn't you listen when I needed help? You said you would help; you said you would answer prayers. Yet when I beg you for help, nothing happens."

What is Habakkuk's second (implied) question for God?

"Violence is everywhere!" I cry,
  but you do not come to save.
HABAKKUK 1:2

_____

_____

_____

How many times have we been there too? We tell God, "There's injustice and sin and evil all around me. I'm asking you to step in and get involved, but you don't. Why, God? Why do you let such bad things happen in the world?"

What is Habakkuk's third question for God?

Must I forever see these evil deeds?
  Why must I watch all this misery?
HABAKKUK 1:3

_____

_____

_____

Many of us have been there—sick of life on this earth, disgusted by the injustice and evil that seem to be running rampant around us. We cry out to God, "Why do you tolerate wrong? Why would you put up with this? I'm sick of it!"

The book of Habakkuk is more than two thousand years old, yet it reads as though it were written today. We can relate to Habakkuk's frustrations and his fight with God.

That's because our world, like Habakkuk's, is crooked. It's bent. It's all backward. And in the midst of this broken world, Habakkuk asks the same question that's on our own lips: "Where are you, God? And what are you doing?"

Answer the following questions honestly, from the place you are with God right now.

Why do you think good people suffer and evil people sometimes prosper?

_____

_____

Why do you think God doesn't always answer prayer?

_____

_____

Why does it sometimes feel like when we do our best for the Lord, we experience the worst from others?

_____

_____

Christians who claim that following God means we won't suffer and have doubts are lying or living in a religious dream world or not experiencing true faith. We can't discover the depths of who God is and grow in our relationship with him until we ponder the problems in the world (like the ones we discussed above).

Anyone who tries to convince you that following Jesus equals being happy all the time might be making it on time to the first service each week, but that person certainly isn't growing up in the faith as God intended. Never mistake shallow optimism for faith.

Habakkuk wasn't a play-it-safe guy or a shallow-faith junkie; he was a risk taker, a bold trailblazer in the faith. And we're about to learn why we want to follow in his daring footsteps.

Day 3

By virtue of being God's image bearers with an inborn sense of justice, we live life repeating, "That's wrong. That's not the way things were meant to be." And whether we're crying out over sticks and stones or bombs or nuclear warfare, the human condition has been broken ever since Adam and Eve sinned—and it always will be.

No matter what injustice we're facing, however, the same truth that Habakkuk discovered all those years ago holds for us now: the questions don't matter nearly as much as the answers.

The LORD replied,

"Look around at the nations;
    look and be amazed!
For I am doing something in your own day,
    something you wouldn't believe
    even if someone told you about it."

HABAKKUK 1:5

In your own words, write God's response to Habakkuk's questions.

_____

_____

Habakkuk: God, do something.
God: I will. I will.
Habakkuk: God, are you sick of these injustices?

God: Yep, I'm sick of it all. I've reached my limit. You think you're frustrated, Habakkuk? Imagine being as holy as I am, with every offense that angers you ultimately being an offense against me. But as always, I have a plan.

Reread Habakkuk 1:6-11.

I am raising up the Babylonians,
    a cruel and violent people.
They will march across the world
    and conquer other lands.
They are notorious for their cruelty
    and do whatever they like.
Their horses are swifter than cheetahs
    and fiercer than wolves at dusk.
Their charioteers charge from far away.
    Like eagles, they swoop down to devour their prey.

On they come, all bent on violence.
    Their hordes advance like a desert wind,
    sweeping captives ahead of them like sand.
They scoff at kings and princes
    and scorn all their fortresses.
They simply pile ramps of earth
    against their walls and capture them!
They sweep past like the wind
    and are gone.
But they are deeply guilty,
    for their own strength is their god.

What group of people is God raising up?

_____

_____

What words and phrases does God use to describe these people?

_____

_____

What is their purpose as they advance?

_____

_____

What is God's verdict about these people?

_____

_____

The Babylonians were a ruthless and evil enemy; there was nothing a human army could have done to stop them. But as cruel as they were, God intended to use them for his purpose. Habakkuk could barely contain this information; he couldn't understand why God would allow such a thing.

When Habakkuk asked God to do something about the unfairness around him, God said, *Okay. How about justice?*

But this wasn't the answer Habakkuk had been expecting. He'd been hoping for national revival, but instead God gave him a declaration of war against his people.

In Habakkuk's opinion, God's answer was no answer at all! In fact, his response only created more questions for Habakkuk.

Read Habakkuk 1:12-17.

O Lord my God, my Holy One, you who are eternal—
      surely you do not plan to wipe us out?
O Lord, our Rock, you have sent these Babylonians to correct us,
      to punish us for our many sins.
But you are pure and cannot stand the sight of evil.
      Will you wink at their treachery?
Should you be silent while the wicked
      swallow up people more righteous than they?

Are we only fish to be caught and killed?
      Are we only sea creatures that have no leader?
Must we be strung up on their hooks
      and caught in their nets while they rejoice and celebrate?
Then they will worship their nets
      and burn incense in front of them.

"These nets are the gods who have made us rich!"
    they will claim.
Will you let them get away with this forever?
    Will they succeed forever in their heartless conquests?

In your own words, write a summary of Habakkuk's rebuttal to God's answer.

_____

_____

    Suddenly this national crisis became a personal crisis of faith for Habakkuk. Yet God still allowed the prophet to wrestle with him and ask the tough questions. God knew that such wrestling gives faith muscles a chance to grow.

    This week, as we continue to trace Habakkuk's faith journey, let's take this truth to heart: if we avoid tough questions, we will remain childish in our faith. But when we choose to be honest with the Lord and talk things out with him, we will grow in the truth of what it really means to have faith. Then, like Habakkuk, we will manage to hold on to that faith, even amid the tough questions.

Day 4

Jesus knows firsthand what it's like to encounter injustice—and to remain absolutely faithful in the midst of it. He doesn't look at our suffering from afar and simply tell us to deal with it. No, he has experienced the same things himself.

Some two thousand years ago, Jesus took on human flesh and became a man. Of all the places we might expect God to go, planet Earth would be among the least likely because of the mess that we've created here. And yet God came.

Jesus was tempted in every way we are but was without sin (see Hebrews 4:15). He was mocked, beaten, scorned, lied to, and betrayed by the people closest to him. The courts that were supposed to bring justice only ran him through a series of false trials. One of the friends who had committed to follow him betrayed him for thirty pieces of silver. His chosen leader, Peter, denied he even knew him. And then he went to the cross—not for his own sake, but for ours. As it says in 2 Corinthians 5:21, "God made Christ, who never sinned, to be the offering for our sin, so that we could be made right with God through Christ."

Jesus died for all our sins—past, present, and future. He rose again to conquer the enemies of sin and death. He gives us new life and, along with it, a new appetite for the things of God rather than the things of this world. He gives us a desire for life, not death; for holiness, not rebellion. And God causes us to hunger and thirst for righteousness so that, like Habakkuk, we become frustrated and sick of the rebellion and sin in the world.

Jesus makes this promise:

God blesses those who hunger and thirst for justice,
    for they will be satisfied.

MATTHEW 5:6

Injustice exists all around us. Think of one news headline this week that serves as an example of the injustice in this world.

_____

_____

If anyone ever had a right to be fed up with the injustice in the world, it was Jesus. His life is a prime example that bad things do happen to good people (or in the case of Jesus, sinless people). Many of us tend to believe that as long as we believe in God, go to church, and read our Bibles, nothing bad will ever happen to us. Yet the book of Habakkuk tells us the truth—tough times are bound to come. Even if we're God's people.

Does God expect more out of people who claim to be Christians?

_____

_____

Read Habakkuk 1:13.

You are pure and cannot stand the sight of evil.
    Will you wink at their treachery?
Should you be silent while the wicked
    swallow up people more righteous than they?

What does Habakkuk seem to be asking God?

_____

_____

Basically Habakkuk was saying, "God, you are so good! How could you let the bad guys win?"

Can you relate to Habakkuk's questions? Have you ever felt like the bad guys always win? Explain how you have seen this played out in your own life or in the lives of those you love.

_____

_____

I think we can agree that Habakkuk was feeling pretty frustrated at this point, with questions that seemed to have no end. But we need to take note of something he said amid those questions:

> I will climb up to my watchtower
> and stand at my guardpost.
> There I will wait to see what the LORD says
> and how he will answer my complaint.

HABAKKUK 2:1

Where did Habakkuk go? What did he do there?

_____

_____

Habakkuk offers a great example for us here. He had questions, he was frustrated, and he didn't understand God, so what did he do? He waited for God to answer.

I submit to you that when we react as Habakkuk does—asking instead of accusing—we are being faithful. What Habakkuk basically says is, "God, here are my questions. You know the answers, so I will just sit here and wait patiently until you tell me what you want me to do. And whatever you say, whatever you want—that's fine with me." Now that's true faith.

Habakkuk's response echoes the response of Asaph the psalmist in Psalm 73. Asaph was wrestling with trusting God as he watched evil people prosper while good people suffered. But somehow, as he poured out his questions to God, he managed to keep things in perspective by choosing to remain in God's presence.

> As for me, I almost lost my footing.
> My feet were slipping, and I was almost gone.
> For I envied the proud
> when I saw them prosper despite their wickedness.
> They seem to live such painless lives;
> their bodies are so healthy and strong.
> They don't have troubles like other people;
> they're not plagued with problems like everyone else.
> They wear pride like a jeweled necklace
> and clothe themselves with cruelty.

These fat cats have everything
    their hearts could ever wish for!
They scoff and speak only evil;
    in their pride they seek to crush others.
They boast against the very heavens,
    and their words strut throughout the earth.
And so the people are dismayed and confused,
    drinking in all their words.
"What does God know?" they ask.
    "Does the Most High even know what's happening?"
Look at these wicked people—
    enjoying a life of ease while their riches multiply.

Did I keep my heart pure for nothing?
    Did I keep myself innocent for no reason?
I get nothing but trouble all day long;
    every morning brings me pain.

If I had really spoken this way to others,
    I would have been a traitor to your people.
So I tried to understand why the wicked prosper.
    But what a difficult task it is!
Then I went into your sanctuary, O God,
    and I finally understood the destiny of the wicked.

PSALM 73:2-17

According to the last verse, where does Asaph go?

_____

_____

_____

It's rare to hear a word from God in the midst of all our noise. Both Habakkuk and Asaph are brilliant examples of how we are to respond to the big wrestlings of our faith—by entering God's presence and listening. It's only then that we are reminded who God is—and who we are in him.

I realized that my heart was bitter,
    and I was all torn up inside.
I was so foolish and ignorant—
    I must have seemed like a senseless animal to you.
Yet I still belong to you;
    you hold my right hand.
You guide me with your counsel,
    leading me to a glorious destiny.
Whom have I in heaven but you?
    I desire you more than anything on earth.
My health may fail, and my spirit may grow weak,
    but God remains the strength of my heart;
    he is mine forever.

Those who desert him will perish,
    for you destroy those who abandon you.
But as for me, how good it is to be near God!
    I have made the Sovereign LORD my shelter,
    and I will tell everyone about the wonderful things you do.

PSALM 73:21-28

Place a check next to the following distractions that keep you away from entering God's presence and prevent you from listening to him.

my emotions toward another person (☐ bitterness, ☐ judgment, ☐ confusion,
    ☐ anger, ☐ unforgiveness)
my feelings toward myself (☐ guilt, ☐ shame, ☐ fear of God's response to me)
the media (☐ TV, ☐ Internet, ☐ social networking)
my schedule (☐ work, ☐ school, ☐ home responsibilities, ☐ church/community
    commitments)
other: _____

God's answer to us may be *wait*, but he wants us to remain connected to him in the midst of the waiting—not just so we can hear the next steps he has for us, but also so that our relationship with him will be deepened in the waiting. If the other noises around us are too loud, they'll drown out his voice until we feel far away. So we must quiet those voices and come into God's presence daily.

We must never discount the wrestling in our waiting. God develops us through the waiting process, not when we arrive on the other side; he grows us through the valley, not on the mountaintop. The waiting doesn't mean God is not moving—Jesus is continually intervening for us and constantly pursuing us. But he knows there is no better way to discover what we truly believe than in the midst of our waiting.

It's never a question of whether God will answer us. He will—always and every time. But not always in the time frame we expect.

Let's join Habakkuk at the watchtower and do something we may not have done in a long time. Let's listen.

Day 5

We may be ready to listen to God, but how do we know what he's trying to say to us? Let's return to Habakkuk's story and see what he discovered.

Read God's response to Habakkuk.

The LORD said to me,

"Write my answer plainly on tablets,
so that a runner can carry the correct message to others.
HABAKKUK 2:2

Did the Lord answer Habakkuk? Absolutely. His response to the prophet was, "Write."

"Write this down, Habakkuk," God said. "I want people to read this one day."

Now take a look at Habakkuk 2:3.

This vision is for a future time.
It describes the end, and it will be fulfilled.
If it seems slow in coming, wait patiently,
for it will surely take place.
It will not be delayed.

When God talks about a "future time," what do you think he's referring to?

_____

_____

That's right—we're part of that future right now!

We are studying the very words of God that Habakkuk received on the watchtower that day. As we read the book named for him, we have the opportunity to sit quietly beside him as we receive a direct, relevant word from the Lord that speaks straight to our hearts as well.

When we read God's Word, we are hearing from God. You and I have the same opportunity Habakkuk had that day, because just as the Spirit of God inspired the writing, the Spirit of God also illuminates our understanding of that writing.

So often we make things more complicated than they need to be, but in reality, the only worthwhile answers to our overwhelming questions are found in his Word.

We don't need a lot more information; we need a lot more faith.

We don't need to know the future; we just need to trust what we already know—that God is faithful.

I have heard all about you, LORD.
  I am filled with awe by your amazing works.
In this time of our deep need,
  help us again as you did in years gone by.
And in your anger,
  remember your mercy.

HABAKKUK 3:2

To live in faith means to trust God's Word no matter how we may feel, what we may experience, or what the consequences might be. Great heroes of faith accomplish extraordinary things in this life because they trust God and do exactly what he tells them to do—against all odds. Champions of faith are not exempt from pain, trials, questions, and suffering. The difference is that instead of giving up on God when suffering hits, they sit quietly on their watchtower, heeding the Word of the Lord.

Champions of faith can proclaim alongside Habakkuk:

Even though the fig trees have no blossoms,
  and there are no grapes on the vines;

even though the olive crop fails,
    and the fields lie empty and barren;
even though the flocks die in the fields,
    and the cattle barns are empty,
yet I will rejoice in the LORD!
    I will be joyful in the God of my salvation!
The Sovereign LORD is my strength!
    He makes me as surefooted as a deer,
    able to tread upon the heights.

HABAKKUK 3:17-19

What "even thoughs" are you facing right now? For you, it might be the bank accounts, not the olive fields, that are barren. It might be seats around the dinner table, not the cattle barns, that are empty. It might be your emotions, not the grapevines, that are fragile and brittle.

Whatever your situation, you may be facing something that requires you to trust God "even though." I encourage you to personalize this passage and fill in the blanks with your own life circumstances.

Even though _____,
    and there are no _____;
even though the _____ fails,
    and the _____ are empty and barren;
even though the _____ die,
    and the _____ are empty,
yet I will rejoice in the LORD!
    I will be joyful in the God of my salvation!
The Sovereign LORD is my strength!
    He makes me as surefooted as a deer,
    able to tread upon the heights.

Questions for Group Discussion or Personal Reflection

1. What are your impressions of the prophet Habakkuk and how he interacted with God? Was there anything about him that surprised you?

   _____

   _____

2. Could you relate to Habakkuk in any way? If so, how? If not, why not?

   _____

   _____

3. Give some examples of times in your life when you've been frustrated with God. How did you interact with him during those seasons of frustration?

   _____

   _____

   _____

   _____

4. Habakkuk learned to communicate with God during times of great stress, doubt, and fear. After studying Habakkuk's life, what new insights do you have about how you can talk to God?

   _____

   _____

5. What are some ways you currently deal with stress, doubt, and fear? Which of those are godly and effective, and which are unhealthy? Are there some habits that could be replaced with more biblical ones (perhaps inspired by Habakkuk's life)?

   _____

   _____

6. Share about a time you had to wait on God. What was that experience like?

_____

_____

_____

_____

7. Read Isaiah 30:18. What benefits can come from waiting on God?

_____

_____

8. How does the world view waiting? How does this compare to a godly understanding of waiting?

_____

_____

9. What do you think it means to be active in our waiting? How can we "be still" and trust him while at the same time not stagnating in our faith?

_____

_____

10. What are you waiting for right now? How do you think God may be working in you through this season?

_____

_____

_____

_____

Week 4

Prayers of Desperation

There have been moments in my life that I regret—moments of shame I've felt because of the pain I caused other people. There have been seasons when the tide of guilt over my foolish choices pulled me further away from God. I kept replaying my rebellion in my mind, questioning why a good and holy God would continue to love me and woo me back despite my filth.

The prayers I offered to God during those moments were certainly cries of desperation, but not the good kind. My desperation stemmed from a sense of "Oh, God, what have I done? Please don't abandon me." In those moments my pleas came not from the gut-wrenching beauty of conviction but from the stench-filled pothole of condemnation. Perhaps you've been there too.

This week we'll discuss another kind of desperation that doesn't stem from sinful rebellion. When our prayers are offered up from a place of deep need, they are pleasing aromas to the Lord. He delights when his children acknowledge that we need him more than our very breath and when we give him his rightful room to work in our lives.

Sometimes God shows himself bigger than we ever believed him to be. Some days, such as the dark days of my chemotherapy treatments, our prayers of silent desperation are all we have to cling to. These prayers are almost painful. They're prayers we wish we didn't have to pray, prayers that barely quench the thirst of souls that are panting desperately for intervention from an almighty, sovereign Creator.

It's in the midst of these prayers that we uncover deep, genuine faith.

This is also the place where God's greatest and most brilliant revelations await us.

Day 1

Let's begin today's study by reading about a woman who was practically the definition of desperate prayer.

> There was a man named Elkanah who lived in Ramah in the region of Zuph in the hill country of Ephraim. He was the son of Jeroham, son of Elihu, son of Tohu, son of Zuph, of Ephraim. Elkanah had two wives, Hannah and Peninnah. Peninnah had children, but Hannah did not.
>
> Each year Elkanah would travel to Shiloh to worship and sacrifice to the LORD of Heaven's Armies at the Tabernacle. The priests of the LORD at that time were the two sons of Eli—Hophni and Phinehas. On the days Elkanah presented his sacrifice, he would give portions of the meat to Peninnah and each of her children. And though he loved Hannah, he would give her only one choice portion because the LORD had given her no children. So Peninnah would taunt Hannah and make fun of her because the LORD had kept her from having children. Year after year it was the same—Peninnah would taunt Hannah as they went to the Tabernacle. Each time, Hannah would be reduced to tears and would not even eat.
>
> "Why are you crying, Hannah?" Elkanah would ask. "Why aren't you eating? Why be downhearted just because you have no children? You have me—isn't that better than having ten sons?"

I SAMUEL I:I-8

How did Hannah's husband feel toward her?

_____

_____

So if Hannah's trouble wasn't being caused by her husband, who seemed to be instigating the problems?

_____

_____

In what ways did this woman cause Hannah trouble?

_____

_____

Based on this narrative, what do we sense about the duration of Hannah's trouble?

_____

_____

How did Hannah's husband respond to her during her season of suffering?

_____

_____

Once after a sacrificial meal at Shiloh, Hannah got up and went to pray. Eli the priest was sitting at his customary place beside the entrance of the Tabernacle. Hannah was in deep anguish, crying bitterly as she prayed to the LORD. And she made this vow: "O LORD of Heaven's Armies, if you will look upon my sorrow and answer my prayer and give me a son, then I will give him back to you. He will be yours for his entire lifetime, and as a sign that he has been dedicated to the LORD, his hair will never be cut."

As she was praying to the LORD, Eli watched her. Seeing her lips moving but hearing no sound, he thought she had been drinking. "Must you come here drunk?" he demanded. "Throw away your wine!"

"Oh no, sir!" she replied. "I haven't been drinking wine or anything stronger. But I am very discouraged, and I was pouring out my heart to the LORD. Don't think I am a wicked woman! For I have been praying out of great anguish and sorrow."

"In that case," Eli said, "go in peace! May the God of Israel grant the request you have asked of him."

"Oh, thank you, sir!" she exclaimed. Then she went back and began to eat again, and she was no longer sad.

The entire family got up early the next morning and went to worship the LORD once more. Then they returned home to Ramah. When Elkanah slept with Hannah, the LORD remembered her plea, and in due time she gave birth to a son. She named him Samuel, for she said, "I asked the LORD for him."
I SAMUEL 1:9-20

How did Hannah respond to her sorrow, both emotionally and physically?

_____

_____

What specifically did Hannah ask the Lord to notice?

_____

_____

What promise did Hannah make to the Lord?

_____

_____

Hannah was so caught up in her prayer of desperation that the priest made what accusation against her?

_____

_____

The truth is, God could have shown up at any point in Hannah's life. He could have opened her womb and caused her to have three or four babies by the time she got "drunk on prayer." He could have intervened by causing her hateful "sister-wife," Peninnah, to come down with a sudden case of laryngitis. He could have caused Hannah's heart to soften to the soothing words of her husband enough that she ceased begging for a baby. God could have handled Mrs. Hannah however he wanted.

And apparently God chose to hear Hannah's prayer of desperation. But then again, he always had heard her prayers.

You see, I believe that Hannah had prayed to God many times over the course of her life. I believe that she'd probably pleaded with him for years to bless her with a child. I also believe that each time she prayed, she grew more desperate for her Lord.

And each time Hannah prayed, the Lord inhaled her sweet perfume and was pleased.

But he knew something Hannah did not.

The more desperate our prayer, the deeper our faith.

Journal your most recent prayer of desperation. Perhaps, like Hannah, you desperately long for a child. Or maybe you are longing for the return of a wayward child. Maybe you're desperate to get a job, to get married, or to recover a lost relationship. Perhaps you've been waiting for what seems like a lifetime for God's intervention.

_____

_____

_____

_____

As you prayed these prayers you wished you'd never had to pray, how did you respond—physically and emotionally? Like Hannah, were you in "deep anguish"? Were you "crying bitterly"?

_____

_____

God reveals his greatest blessings when his people begin to pray.

Prayer that deepens and widens our faith can't be taught or practiced or repeated until we have all the words just perfect. Prayer that changes our lives is borne out of our desperation. And the longer we feel a hole in our lives, the more desperate and consistent our prayer life should become.

The heavier the need, the deeper the faith. And the greater the blessing.

Day 2

When we tell ourselves that we *should* pray, we quickly run out of desire. Any motivation built on the "I should" or "I ought to" or "I need to" platform will soon crumble, for there is no human will strong enough or holy enough to pursue prayer based on its own strength.

Prayer isn't something we must do to honor God. In fact, God doesn't need our prayers to make him more honorable. It isn't the Father who needs the input of his children, but the children who need the wise direction of their Father. God pushes us into desperate times so that we can experience deeper communication with him.

If life is easy, our prayers are easy too—sugarcoated words that come from a sense of *I should pray because it's the right thing to do.*

For example, a friend corners you at the grocery store and replays her current distress. The easy response is to say, "I'll pray for you." Or maybe you sit down to a meal with your family after church. Your mom gives you the squinty eyes and the nod from across the table, so you say, "Hey, guys, let me bless our food."

When I was going through my chemo treatments, whenever I showed up anywhere in my head wrap, perfect strangers would walk up to me, grab my arm, and say, "I'll be praying for you," without even asking my name.

Who knows—maybe they really did add me to their prayer list. And maybe when you tell someone you'll be praying for him or her, you really mean it, and when you bless the food, you do it out of a true desire to thank God for your meal. The point is, though, it's one thing to say the words that we'll pray; it's another thing to actually do it. And perhaps the bigger question is, *where* are we praying from? Is it just lip service, or do our prayers come from a gut level—from a place of desperation?

Read the verses below. Then for each one, describe the circumstances and atmosphere surrounding Jesus as he prayed.

One day when the crowds were being baptized, Jesus himself was baptized. As he was praying, the heavens opened, and the Holy Spirit, in bodily form, descended on him like a dove. And a voice from heaven said, "You are my dearly loved Son, and you bring me great joy."
LUKE 3:21-22

_____

_____

Jesus often withdrew to the wilderness for prayer.
LUKE 5:16

_____

_____

One day soon afterward Jesus went up on a mountain to pray, and he prayed to God all night.
LUKE 6:12

_____

_____

One day Jesus left the crowds to pray alone. Only his disciples were with him, and he asked them, "Who do people say I am?"
LUKE 9:18

_____

_____

About eight days later Jesus took Peter, John, and James up on a mountain to pray. And as he was praying, the appearance of his face was transformed, and his clothes became dazzling white.
LUKE 9:28-29

_____

_____

Once Jesus was in a certain place praying. As he finished, one of his disciples came to him and said, "Lord, teach us to pray, just as John taught his disciples."

LUKE 11:1

_____

_____

The difference between a grocery-store-passing "I'm praying for you" or "Please bless the pot roast" and the prayers described in these verses from Luke is simple: *desperation*. While those less weighty prayers have a place, they don't usually qualify as the kind that deepen our faith and grant us great revelations.

Prayers that radiate from heartfelt needs inside us require sacrifice on our part. Prayers that ache for answers take time, meditation, emotional output, and physical energy on our part—just as they did for Hannah.

When we read about Jesus' prayers in these verses, we see a man who was desperate to know and worship his Father through prayer.

Take this prayer inventory to see where you fall in your desire to know God more through prayer. Place a check next to any of the statements that apply to you right now.

☐ I'm not very faithful about praying. Life is so busy that I rarely think of it.
☐ I pray but not very often. If I'm honest, I mostly pray when I need something or when something in my life goes wrong.
☐ I pray fairly regularly, but I do so because I feel like I ought to so I can be right with God.
☐ I try to pray numerous times throughout the day because I know I need to connect with my Father.
☐ I've never really thought about how prayer might deepen my faith. I pray because it's what I was taught to do.
☐ When I pray, I leave room to hear from God.
☐ I set aside time each day to meditate and pray to God.
☐ I desire to grow in my prayer life and go deeper with God.
☐ I can truly say I'm desperate for God—there is something really difficult I've been bringing before him for a long time now.
☐ Sometimes I feel like I'm praying the same thing over and over again, but

I won't lose heart, because I know he's deepening my faith through my persistence.

Based on your checks on the previous page and above, what is one thing that needs to change in your prayer life for you to become more desperate?

_____

_____

Read this passage to see what Jesus had to say about desperate prayer.

One day Jesus told his disciples a story to show that they should always pray and never give up. "There was a judge in a certain city," he said, "who neither feared God nor cared about people. A widow of that city came to him repeatedly, saying, 'Give me justice in this dispute with my enemy.' The judge ignored her for a while, but finally he said to himself, 'I don't fear God or care about people, but this woman is driving me crazy. I'm going to see that she gets justice, because she is wearing me out with her constant requests!'"
LUKE 18:1-5

What would it look like for you to "pray and never give up"?

_____

_____

Day 3

Let's begin today by rereading 1 Samuel 1:7-8. Keep an eye out for the role of human comfort in this story.

> Year after year it was the same—Peninnah would taunt Hannah as they went to the Tabernacle. Each time, Hannah would be reduced to tears and would not even eat.
> "Why are you crying, Hannah?" Elkanah would ask. "Why aren't you eating? Why be downhearted just because you have no children? You have me—isn't that better than having ten sons?"

Hannah knew her man loved her, but even his kind words were no match for the painful desire inside her to be a mama.

Have you been there? Can you relate to Hannah on some level? You may not be aching for a child, but we all know what it's like to long for something and to feel like God is silent. We know what it's like to be hurting and to have a friend or family member try to offer comforting words and think, *They just don't understand.*

Take a moment to talk to God. Are you there now? When was the last time you thought, *They just don't understand*?

_____

_____

_____

_____

Do you remember the words of encouragement or comfort someone offered to you when you were going through a hard season? Write them here (as best as you remember).

_____

_____

_____

_____

Now write what *you* tend to say to others when they are down or discouraged. (For example, "I'm praying for you" or "Is there anything I can do to help?")

_____

_____

_____

_____

Tender words or genuine prayers from a friend or loved one can certainly lift our spirits when we're down. Not to knock anyone here (because frankly, I'm pretty impressed with dear Elkanah, who wanted to be reason enough for Hannah to smile), but I think you will agree that there are some moments in life when no mortal words seem to help. Especially during moments—or even seasons—of desperation.

And sometimes when God wants us to get serious about stepping up our faith, he intentionally depletes our human resources department. That's because he knows that no other voice, no other words of comfort, no other person can be for us what he alone is.

Read the following verses and then write who God is, what he does, and how he works in ways far beyond all others.

The Holy Spirit produces this kind of fruit in our lives: love, joy, peace, patience, kindness, goodness, faithfulness, gentleness, and self-control. There is no law against these things!
GALATIANS 5:22-23

_____

_____

I am leaving you with a gift—peace of mind and heart. And the peace I give is a gift the world cannot give. So don't be troubled or afraid.

JOHN 14:27

_____

_____

I have told you these things so that you will be filled with my joy. Yes, your joy will overflow!

JOHN 15:11

_____

_____

May God the Father and Christ Jesus our Lord give you grace, mercy, and peace.

1 TIMOTHY 1:2

_____

_____

God will grant us minds and hearts to know him in those desperate moments when we choose his voice—and his voice alone. This is the kind of prayer that changes us, and it's the kind of prayer that can come to us only when we lean in to hear the voice of our Creator.

Only God's Word, through the Holy Spirit, can bring the changes, answers, and revelations we yearn for. When we look to be changed by the words of another mortal we are often disappointed. Human words, after all, carry no power to change our circumstances.

Now, don't get me wrong—I'm not saying we should disconnect from other people or stop speaking truth and hope to them. We should be like Elkanah was with Hannah in her moment of distress. (Can you imagine the night ahead of him if he'd said nothing? Yeesh!) We never know when and to whom God will use our voice to lift the spirits of someone who is hurting, so we should speak love over others boldly and often, as the Lord directs.

My word of caution now is to those of us who are recipients of that encouragement. Never rely on the words of another human being to give you joy, peace, patience, power, or strength, for I assure you that's far too heavy a weight for a person to carry.

Instead, cry out to the one who *is* joy, peace, patience, power, and strength, and ask him to speak directly into your despair. He alone designed your heart, and therefore he's by far the best-qualified voice to soothe it.

Day 4

Let's go back to the story of Hannah, focusing especially on what her prayers were like.

> Once after a sacrificial meal at Shiloh, Hannah got up and went to pray.
> Eli the priest was sitting at his customary place beside the entrance of the
> Tabernacle. Hannah was in deep anguish, crying bitterly as she prayed to the
> Lord. And she made this vow: "O Lord of Heaven's Armies, if you will look
> upon my sorrow and answer my prayer and give me a son, then I will give
> him back to you. He will be yours for his entire lifetime, and as a sign that he
> has been dedicated to the Lord, his hair will never be cut."
>
> 1 SAMUEL 1:9-11

Look again at the first sentence in this passage—it is oh so sweet: "Hannah got up and went to pray."

Notice two important things in this sentence: (1) Hannah knew that hearing from God was a priority, and (2) she knew she wasn't strong enough to hear him clearly from where she sat.

Hannah was determined to hear from the Lord about her deepest and most desperate desire—to have a son. And she knew that if she stayed at dinner or confided in the friend next to her, she would be too distracted to hear from him.

I love this about our dear Hannah. Her priority was not to speak to God; it was to *hear* from him. And she was going to do whatever needed to be done to make that happen!

Hannah's prayer was powerful. It was a promise to God—a commitment to give her son to the Lord.

Yes, Hannah spoke, but I'm convinced that she spent much of her time before the Lord simply listening. If she's anything like the rest of us, I imagine it would have been pretty difficult for her to form words amid her tears anyway. Hannah's speaking and listening came directly out of a heart of sorrow and suffering—a soul laid bare and broken before her Maker.

How does God respond to our broken hearts? Match each psalm with the corresponding answer.

Psalm 34:18	He heals them.
Psalm 51:17	He is close to them.
Psalm 147:3	He will not reject them.

Read Psalm 51:8 and then rewrite it in the space below.

Oh, give me back my joy again;
    you have broken me—
    now let me rejoice.

_____

_____

Sometimes God breaks our hearts for himself.

I know some people will disagree with that statement, but in my own cancer journey, I give God credit for breaking my health, my emotions, my mind, and most certainly my heart during that torturous season. I believe that God desired to draw me to himself in a deeper way than ever before through that anguish, and I believe he did the same for Hannah in her barrenness.

When things are going fine, we don't need God (or at least we don't think we do). When we don't have any problems, we see no reason to draw closer to him. It only makes sense to me that God would break our hearts in order to reach us and pull us beyond the distractions of life and the sinfulness of our flesh.

Write about a time when you believed your pain, anguish, and heartbreak came directly from the hand of the Lord.

_____

_____

_____

_____

What is your reaction when you think about God as a "heartbreaker"?

_____

_____

Some people might be quick to accuse Hannah of bargaining with God in this passage, but I don't think this was the case in context of her time. Bearing a son would be a gift of grace—she knew that full well. But offering up her son to God was an act of sacrifice. Hannah would have her son for only the first three years of his life, and then she would give him up to be a Nazirite (see Numbers 6). It almost seems easier to remain barren than to give up a gift you have so desperately longed for.

But as we will soon learn, Hannah's barrenness and Samuel's birth were all part of God's premeditated plan. He chose to harness his power into the womb of this great prayer warrior.

The name Hannah means "woman of grace." And that she was. For it was grace that caused her to be barren, grace that drove her to desperation, grace that deepened her faith, and grace that ultimately granted her a son.

Day 5

Let's take a look at Hannah's story again—this time through the eyes of Eli the priest.

> As she was praying to the LORD, Eli watched her. Seeing her lips moving but hearing no sound, he thought she had been drinking. "Must you come here drunk?" he demanded. "Throw away your wine!"
>
> "Oh no, sir!" she replied. "I haven't been drinking wine or anything stronger. But I am very discouraged, and I was pouring out my heart to the LORD. Don't think I am a wicked woman! For I have been praying out of great anguish and sorrow."
>
> "In that case," Eli said, "go in peace! May the God of Israel grant the request you have asked of him."
>
> I SAMUEL 1:12-17

Come on, Eli! Don't you know a praying woman when you see one?

When I read this, I hurt for Hannah on a personal level. I know what it's like to be misunderstood by people, especially those in the church. Sometimes people don't know what to do with strong emotion—whether it's passion or pain—so they make assumptions.

Eli was a spiritual leader in his community. But his discernment failed him as he observed Hannah's passionate prayer. He accused Hannah of pouring out too much wine, when in truth she was pouring out her heart before the Lord.

And as much as I would like him to, Eli doesn't apologize. He does, however, give Hannah his blessing. And that was all she needed to pick up her head, take a deep breath, throw her shoulders back, and get her tushy back into dinner.

It hurts when we're misunderstood by others—especially when it comes to our passion for God. Place a check next to all the experiences you've had with being misunderstood.

- ☐ You've been criticized for engaging with the wrong people (e.g., spending time with unbelievers).
- ☐ You've been criticized for the way you worship (e.g., dancing, raising your hands in church).
- ☐ You've been criticized for your personality (e.g., being too internal/meditative or being too social/outgoing).
- ☐ You've been criticized for the career you've pursued.
- ☐ You've been criticized for the person you married.
- ☐ You've been criticized for the way you speak (e.g., too bold, too confident, too passionate).

Hannah would have missed a powerful opportunity to go deeper with God had she given too much thought to what Eli thought of her passion. Instead, we see a peace come over her as though a burden had been lifted—almost as if she already knew God had heard (and answered) her prayer.

When your passion is centered on Christ, hang your head before no one! For you will answer to no one other than Jesus Christ.

Let's read this passage and see what happened to Hannah next.

When the child was weaned, Hannah took him to the Tabernacle in Shiloh. They brought along a three-year-old bull for the sacrifice and a basket of flour and some wine. After sacrificing the bull, they brought the boy to Eli. "Sir, do you remember me?" Hannah asked. "I am the very woman who stood here several years ago praying to the LORD. I asked the LORD to give me this boy, and he has granted my request. Now I am giving him to the LORD, and he will belong to the LORD his whole life." And they worshiped the LORD there.

I SAMUEL 1:24-28

God answered Hannah's prayer—he gave her a son. She named him Samuel, which means "asked" as well as "heard" in Hebrew. So Samuel means "asked of God" and "heard of God." If you were to read about the life of Samuel, you would discover that he was both an answer to prayer and a great man of prayer.

And just as Hannah had promised, she weaned her son and prepared him to live a life of service to the Lord.

I love the mental picture of Hannah returning Samuel to the Tabernacle and reminding Eli (the priest who had thought she was drunk) that she was the woman he had blessed more than three years earlier.

Can you imagine the great faith on the part of Hannah as she passed her beloved son over to a man who had once misread her spiritual passion as drunkenness? As a mother, I feel my stomach turn at the thought. Yet she remained faithful once again through another heartbreaking moment from the hand of the Lord.

Her life, her desperation, her prayers, her devotion, and her faithfulness all reached a climactic moment as she walked away from her treasured son and left him in the hands of her trusted God.

Scripture records Hannah's song of praise:

Then Hannah prayed:

"My heart rejoices in the Lord!
    The Lord has made me strong.
Now I have an answer for my enemies;
    I rejoice because you rescued me.
No one is holy like the Lord!
    There is no one besides you;
    there is no Rock like our God.

"Stop acting so proud and haughty!
    Don't speak with such arrogance!
For the Lord is a God who knows what you have done;
    he will judge your actions.
The bow of the mighty is now broken,
    and those who stumbled are now strong.
Those who were well fed are now starving,
    and those who were starving are now full.
The childless woman now has seven children,
    and the woman with many children wastes away.

The LORD gives both death and life;
    he brings some down to the grave but raises others up.
The LORD makes some poor and others rich;
    he brings some down and lifts others up.
He lifts the poor from the dust
    and the needy from the garbage dump.
He sets them among princes,
    placing them in seats of honor.
For all the earth is the LORD's,
    and he has set the world in order.

"He will protect his faithful ones,
    but the wicked will disappear in darkness.
No one will succeed by strength alone.
    Those who fight against the LORD will be shattered.
He thunders against them from heaven;
    the LORD judges throughout the earth.
He gives power to his king;
    he increases the strength of his anointed one."

1 SAMUEL 2:1-10

Which parts of Hannah's song stand out to you on a personal level?

_____

_____

_____

When prayers are prideful, they rarely end in praise. When prayers are surface level, they rarely end in song.

Hannah was able to walk away praying and singing because she didn't underestimate the power of her God and the purposes he had for her and her son. This is breathtaking to me, because I usually break down in sobs when I merely leave my children with their grandparents for a weekend. Yet here was Hannah, leaving her son for a lifetime, and she walked away in praise.

The world will never understand the partnership of prayer, desperation, and praise. When people see your passion, they will misunderstand it and wonder how you can thank God in times of pain and suffering. But when we choose to believe God has fashioned each one of us for his glory, we can praise him, knowing our trials offer us the opportunity to catch a glimpse of God we've never seen before.

Our faith is deepened when we grow desperate for him in times of brokenness. And like Hannah, our response in those times should be prayer and praise.

Read Luke 1:46-55 for a story about another young woman whose faith was cata-pulted to new heights when God turned her world upside down. She responded in a song of praise much like Hannah's.

Mary responded,

"Oh, how my soul praises the Lord.
    How my spirit rejoices in God my Savior!
For he took notice of his lowly servant girl,
    and from now on all generations will call me blessed.
For the Mighty One is holy,
    and he has done great things for me.
He shows mercy from generation to generation
    to all who fear him.
His mighty arm has done tremendous things!
    He has scattered the proud and haughty ones.
He has brought down princes from their thrones
    and exalted the humble.
He has filled the hungry with good things
    and sent the rich away with empty hands.
He has helped his servant Israel
    and remembered to be merciful.
For he made this promise to our ancestors,
    to Abraham and his children forever."

In the space below, write your own prayer of praise, thanking God for who he is and what he has done for you.

_____

_____

Questions for Group Discussion or Personal Reflection

1. What strikes you about Hannah's story and, in particular, the way she prayed?

   _____

   _____

2. Have you ever prayed a prayer of desperation that stemmed from a deep place of longing, like Hannah's prayer did? What were the circumstances?

   _____

   _____

3. If your son or daughter or a child you love came to you with a request from a place of brokenness and desperate need, how would you feel?

   _____

   _____

4. If human parents hurt alongside their children when they're in pain, how do you think our Creator feels when his children are in pain?

   _____

   _____

5. Under what circumstances in your life are you most likely to pray?

   _____

   _____

6. Under what circumstances are you least likely to pray?

   _____

   _____

7. Psalm 17:6 says, "I am praying to you because I know you will answer, O God. Bend down and listen as I pray." What does it mean to you that God is eager to listen to your prayers?

   _____

   _____

8. Read Psalm 32:7-8. What do you think it means that God is our hiding place?

_____

_____

9. How have you personally experienced God as your hiding place?

_____

_____

10. What would it look like to trust God whatever your circumstances?

_____

_____

Week 5

......

The Storms of Faith

Jesus rarely shows himself to us at the times we think he should.

In fact, there are many times we feel God has completely deserted us—especially when the dark clouds of trouble begin to circle overhead.

Many of the psalms include David's complaints that God seems far away.

The book of Jonah is about a man crying, "Where are you, God?" from inside the belly of a large fish.

The book of Zechariah is devoted to inspiring people who had given up on God when he didn't show himself the way they wanted him to.

And the majority of the New Testament is instructions for Christ followers about how to live joyfully and purposefully despite our greatest fears, doubts, pain, and suffering.

Yet it is in these very moments, when God seems far away, that he is molding within us a deeper faith—a trust that our Creator is always near, working for his glory and our good.

God promises us

When you go through deep waters,
I will be with you.

ISAIAH 43:2

We may not feel that God is present or active just when we think he should be, but we can rest assured that he knows better than we do when we need him to reveal himself. And he will show himself faithful despite our unfaithfulness.

This week we will learn about a man from Scripture who asked the question, Where are you, God? Peter is a prime example of someone who loved the Lord and experienced him intimately, yet still felt the lonely weight of God's perceived absence.

Through Peter's life and interactions with Jesus, we can learn how God develops our faith. And as we will see, great faith is most often developed when we are least expecting or desiring it.

Let's join Peter and the rest of the disciples smack-dab inside a faith-sized storm. The clouds and water were raging, death felt imminent, and Jesus . . . well, this storm was his idea in the first place.

Day 1

The sun was setting on another faith-staggering day for Jesus' disciples.

As the awestruck gang rowed their way toward the banks of Capernaum, they found it hard to stop talking about the five thousand men plus all the women and children who had feasted their fill on fish and bread. To think the disciples had been unsure of what their own lunch would be that day, much less the thousands of people who had gathered to hear Jesus teach!

When they replayed the look on the young boy's face when he gave up his small lunch of five pieces of bread and two fish—well, the disciples could hardly contain their excitement. They were exhausted, but the retelling of the day's miraculous events spread contagious laughter throughout the boat. But that laughter dwindled the moment Andrew caught a glimpse of the perplexed look on his brother's face.

Peter was an expert fisherman, and he knew the sea like the back of his hand. So if Peter looked worried, there was definitely a reason for concern. All lighthearted banter subsided as the disciples began to fret. "What's wrong, Peter? What should we do?"

The wind was picking up, and the waves were growing stronger. Adrenaline-fueled conversations were quickly replaced by adrenaline-fueled chaos as the men began pulling ropes, shifting weight, and arguing with one another.

Then all at once Andrew's attention shifted from the waves that were pulling them out to sea to the fact that a key member of their team was absent.

"Jesus! Where's Jesus?" Andrew shouted. "He should be with us right now!"

Our "trials by storm" often hit us directly after great moments of victory or celebration. Can you think of a time this has been true for you? Describe the victory you experienced and then describe the storm that came soon after.

My Victory	My Storm
_____	_____
_____	_____
_____	_____
_____	_____

As you think about the storm you went through, what seemed contrary to the way you thought Jesus should work? Perhaps, like the disciples, you felt Jesus should have been guiding the boat—or at least in the boat with you—but instead he was out walking on the water.

_____

_____

Read Matthew 14:22-24.

Immediately after this, Jesus insisted that his disciples get back into the boat and cross to the other side of the lake, while he sent the people home. After sending them home, he went up into the hills by himself to pray. Night fell while he was there alone.

Meanwhile, the disciples were in trouble far away from land, for a strong wind had risen, and they were fighting heavy waves.

Why wasn't Jesus in the boat as the storm pushed the boat farther from the shore?

_____

_____

Read John 6:14-15 for more background on why Jesus quickly excused himself after feeding the five thousand.

When the people saw him do this miraculous sign, they exclaimed, "Surely, he is the Prophet we have been expecting!" When Jesus saw that they were ready to force him to be their king, he slipped away into the hills by himself.

Why did Jesus retreat to pray?

_____

_____

John records that Jesus was in a hurry to dismiss the crowd and get the disciples back to the boat so he could get some quality time with his Father. Jesus knew the motives of the crowds—they were looking for Jesus to meet their own desires, not seeking God's will.

The difficult yet beautiful truth about this story is that Jesus knew a storm was coming long before he instructed the disciples to go out on the lake without him. Yet he sent his disciples directly into the storm—alone.

Why do you think Jesus sent them into the storm without him?

_____

_____

We may think we understand why God has placed us somewhere or sent us to a certain place. And while God may reveal some things in the moment, a true storm of revelation keeps working on our faith long after the rain ceases. God can use our faith storms to do a work in our relationships, our emotions, our thought patterns, and our spiritual maturity.

God sees the big picture of our lives, not merely the individual pieces, as we do. The disciples simply thought Jesus had missed the boat, when in reality, Jesus was waiting for the full measure of their faith to be tested.

So how did their faith measure up? We'll find out in day 2.

Day 2

The disciples were beginning to panic in the midst of the howling wind and the treacherous rocking of the boat. Then someone shouted, "What's that?"

Everybody aboard froze. No one could move as each man's gaze fixed on the dark form that was now moving toward them.

Fear rippled through the vessel as the foreboding presence drew closer and closer to the edge of the boat. They begged Peter to turn around. "It's a ghost!" someone cried.

Suddenly, a familiar voice resonated within their hearts and minds. It's doubtful they could have physically heard the voice above the howling wind and crashing waves, but the voice was certainly inside them—making its way from their hearts into their nervous systems and then to their brains, sending a message like a whisper to their souls.

The voice was warm and tender, immediately soothing their fear, worry, and anxiety: "Don't be afraid. . . . Take courage. I am here!" (Matthew 14:27).

Read the following passages. In the blanks, write *who* God was telling not to be afraid and *what* he was commanding them not to be afraid of.

Jacob set out for Egypt with all his possessions. And when he came to Beersheba, he offered sacrifices to the God of his father, Isaac. During the night God spoke to him in a vision. "Jacob! Jacob!" he called.

"Here I am," Jacob replied.

"I am God, the God of your father," the voice said. "Do not be afraid to go down to Egypt, for there I will make your family into a great nation."

GENESIS 46:1-3

Who:

_____

What:

_____

_____

After the death of Moses the LORD's servant, the LORD spoke to Joshua son of Nun, Moses' assistant. He said, "Moses my servant is dead. Therefore, the time has come for you to lead these people, the Israelites, across the Jordan River into the land I am giving them. . . . This is my command—be strong and courageous! Do not be afraid or discouraged. For the LORD your God is with you wherever you go."

JOSHUA 1:1-2, 9

Who:

_____

What:

_____

_____

One night the king of Aram sent a great army with many chariots and horses to surround the city.

When the servant of the man of God got up early the next morning and went outside, there were troops, horses, and chariots everywhere. "Oh, sir, what will we do now?" the young man cried to Elisha.

"Don't be afraid!" Elisha told him. "For there are more on our side than on theirs!" Then Elisha prayed, "O LORD, open his eyes and let him see!" The LORD opened the young man's eyes, and when he looked up, he saw that the hillside around Elisha was filled with horses and chariots of fire.

2 KINGS 6:14-17

Who:

_____

What:

_____

_____

Early on Sunday morning, as the new day was dawning, Mary Magdalene and the other Mary went out to visit the tomb.

Suddenly there was a great earthquake! For an angel of the Lord came down from heaven, rolled aside the stone, and sat on it. His face shone like lightning, and his clothing was as white as snow. The guards shook with fear when they saw him, and they fell into a dead faint.

Then the angel spoke to the women. "Don't be afraid!" he said. "I know you are looking for Jesus, who was crucified."

MATTHEW 28:1-5

Who:

_____

What:

_____

_____

As gale-force winds continued to batter the ship, the crew began throwing the cargo overboard. The following day they even took some of the ship's gear and threw it overboard. The terrible storm raged for many days, blotting out the sun and the stars, until at last all hope was gone.

No one had eaten for a long time. Finally, Paul called the crew together and said, "Men, you should have listened to me in the first place and not left Crete. You would have avoided all this damage and loss. But take courage! None of you will lose your lives, even though the ship will go down. For last night an angel of the God to whom I belong and whom I serve stood beside me, and he said, 'Don't be afraid, Paul, for you will surely stand trial before Caesar! What's more, God in his goodness has granted safety to everyone sailing with you.'"

ACTS 27:18-24

Who:

_____

_____

What:

_____

_____

Write about a time when you felt God's voice warm you and cover you with peace. Have you ever sensed God telling you, "Do not be afraid"?

_____

_____

We must never judge our safety and security on our circumstances.

Many of us have the false assumption that just because we're in the boat with God, we'll be guaranteed smooth sailing ahead. But remember, Jesus told the disciples to get into the boat, knowing a storm was in their future. God's desire for us in the midst of our storms is always to draw us closer to himself.

The Bible gives us examples of two different types of storms we may find ourselves in.

Read Jonah 1:1-16.

The LORD gave this message to Jonah son of Amittai: "Get up and go to the great city of Nineveh. Announce my judgment against it because I have seen how wicked its people are."

But Jonah got up and went in the opposite direction to get away from the LORD. He went down to the port of Joppa, where he found a ship leaving for Tarshish. He bought a ticket and went on board, hoping to escape from the LORD by sailing to Tarshish.

But the LORD hurled a powerful wind over the sea, causing a violent storm that threatened to break the ship apart. Fearing for their lives, the desperate sailors shouted to their gods for help and threw the cargo overboard to lighten the ship.

But all this time Jonah was sound asleep down in the hold. So the captain went down after him. "How can you sleep at a time like this?" he shouted.

"Get up and pray to your god! Maybe he will pay attention to us and spare our lives."

Then the crew cast lots to see which of them had offended the gods and caused the terrible storm. When they did this, the lots identified Jonah as the culprit. "Why has this awful storm come down on us?" they demanded. "Who are you? What is your line of work? What country are you from? What is your nationality?"

Jonah answered, "I am a Hebrew, and I worship the LORD, the God of heaven, who made the sea and the land."

The sailors were terrified when they heard this, for he had already told them he was running away from the LORD. "Oh, why did you do it?" they groaned. And since the storm was getting worse all the time, they asked him, "What should we do to you to stop this storm?"

"Throw me into the sea," Jonah said, "and it will become calm again. I know that this terrible storm is all my fault."

Instead, the sailors rowed even harder to get the ship to the land. But the stormy sea was too violent for them, and they couldn't make it. Then they cried out to the LORD, Jonah's God. "O LORD," they pleaded, "don't make us die for this man's sin. And don't hold us responsible for his death. O LORD, you have sent this storm upon him for your own good reasons."

Then the sailors picked Jonah up and threw him into the raging sea, and the storm stopped at once! The sailors were awestruck by the LORD's great power, and they offered him a sacrifice and vowed to serve him.

What are the main events recorded in this passage?

_____

_____

Now read the whole story about the disciples in the storm.

Immediately after this, Jesus insisted that his disciples get back into the boat and cross to the other side of the lake, while he sent the people home. After sending them home, he went up into the hills by himself to pray. Night fell while he was there alone.

Meanwhile, the disciples were in trouble far away from land, for a strong wind had risen, and they were fighting heavy waves. About three o'clock in the morning Jesus came toward them, walking on the water. When the disciples saw him walking on the water, they were terrified. In their fear, they cried out, "It's a ghost!"

But Jesus spoke to them at once. "Don't be afraid," he said. "Take courage. I am here!"

Then Peter called to him, "Lord, if it's really you, tell me to come to you, walking on the water."

"Yes, come," Jesus said.

So Peter went over the side of the boat and walked on the water toward Jesus. But when he saw the strong wind and the waves, he was terrified and began to sink. "Save me, Lord!" he shouted.

Jesus immediately reached out and grabbed him. "You have so little faith," Jesus said. "Why did you doubt me?"

When they climbed back into the boat, the wind stopped. Then the disciples worshiped him. "You really are the Son of God!" they exclaimed.

MATTHEW 14:22-33

What are the main events recorded in this passage?

_____

_____

Note that the reason for each of these storms was different. Jonah was in a storm of *correction*, while the boys following Jesus were in a storm of *perfection*. Jonah's storm resulted from his own disobedience. He had sinned and rebelled against the Lord, and now the Lord was using the storm to correct him, discipline him, and bring him back to himself. The disciples, in contrast, got into the boat as an act of obedience. Yet the Lord's desire was to take them deeper still—further into the waters of faith. Jonah had to be corrected; the disciples had to be perfected.

But even though the purpose behind these storms differed, the desired result remained the same: deeper faith.

Both were storms of faith—and storms of faith are never easy. Perhaps the most difficult part of all when we find ourselves in the wind and waves is staying fixed on the one who made the storm in the first place.

Day 3

It sounded like Jesus—a voice they'd all grown fond of throughout their months of traveling together. "Don't be afraid," he said. "Take courage. I am here!" Yet it seemed like Jesus was nowhere to be found.

He wasn't in the corner of the boat, curled up sleeping as he sometimes did. He wasn't perched at the front of the boat, grinning, eyes closed, allowing the breeze to rush into his face. And he wasn't making jokes with the guys, laughing until his sides hurt.

Once again Jesus showed his love for them, but this time it wasn't from inside the boat.

Read Matthew 14:26.

When the disciples saw him walking on the water, they were terrified. In their fear, they cried out, "It's a ghost!"

Write the first half of this verse below.

_____

_____

Did you catch that? Jesus was walking on the water!

I picture Peter motioning for everyone to be quiet and for the rowers to stop as his eyes strained forward and he leaned out over the water.

Sure enough, it was Jesus.

As the company of men stood speechless, awestruck, and paralyzed, Peter couldn't contain himself. "Peter called to him, 'Lord, if it's really you, tell me to come to you, walking on the water'" (Matthew 14:28). All eyes jolted from the dark shadow in front of them and onto Peter.

Peter never looked at them. Careful but determined, he hitched up his robe and clenched it tightly in one hand. He swung one leg over the side and then the other until he was perched on the edge.

And then, in a move that evoked a collective gasp from his friends, Peter dropped the weight of his entire body and stood on the surface of the water.

Without breaking his gaze, Peter took one step and then another, growing more confident with each step toward Jesus. Meanwhile, the guys on the boat held their breath.

Peter's heart was racing and his adrenaline was pumping as his feet propelled him forward. With each step, he drew nearer to the one he loved. The face of his dearest friend and teacher was becoming clear. Peter's stride lengthened and his face brightened when he saw that Jesus was only a few feet in front of him. Peter couldn't help but feel overwhelmed by an even deeper love for Jesus, and a gust of supernatural joy burst out of him in a half laugh, half cry.

At some point he noticed the waves lapping at his calves and the wind whipping around him. No doubt they had been there all along, but he had been so focused on Jesus that he hadn't noticed them. Now he couldn't get his mind off them. They shook his gaze, and in an instant, Peter blinked.

Read what happened to Peter next.

When he saw the strong wind and the waves, he was terrified and began to sink. "Save me, Lord!" he shouted.

MATTHEW 14:30

Why did Peter start to sink?

_____

_____

_____

The Bible never says Peter took his eyes off Jesus. However, he was distracted by the wind and the waves in his periphery, and it was just enough to tempt him to break his focus.

Place a check next to the distractions that tempt you to shift your focus away from Jesus. (Check all that apply.)

☐ my busy schedule
☐ the needs of other people
☐ the demands of my job
☐ the demands of my studies/school
☐ social commitments
☐ phone, e-mail, Internet, social media, etc.
☐ a dysfunctional or strained relationship
☐ my marriage
☐ my rebellious child
☐ my anger toward someone
☐ my bitterness toward someone

Sometimes our greatest storms, trials, fears, and doubts come when we're looking smack-dab into the face of Jesus. In the same moment we love Jesus, we're capable of choosing doubt and sin.

Describe a time you were walking with your eyes on Jesus and then you found yourself sinking. What distractions contributed to your taking your eyes off Jesus?

_____

_____

_____

If you feel like you're sinking, you're in good company. But don't lose heart—there's hope for all of us, just as there was for Peter.

Day 4

So why do godly people—even someone like Peter who was one of Jesus' close friends—do ungodly things? Why do people who love Jesus still sink?

The short answer to this question is that we are people in continual conflict. Take a look at this passage to see what the Bible has to say about this:

We know that God's children do not make a practice of sinning, for God's Son holds them securely, and the evil one cannot touch them. We know that we are children of God and that the world around us is under the control of the evil one.

And we know that the Son of God has come, and he has given us understanding so that we can know the true God. And now we live in fellowship with the true God because we live in fellowship with his Son, Jesus Christ. He is the only true God, and he is eternal life.

1 JOHN 5:18-20

One of the most captivating pieces of these verses is the phrase "the world around us is under the control of the evil one." I don't know about you, but this truth sounds devastating to me. At first glance, it might sound like there's no way for us to win, but we'll go deeper than a swift glance.

Read the following verses, and write what God says about our interactions with the world.

Jesus gave his life for our sins, just as God our Father planned, in order to rescue us from this evil world in which we live.
GALATIANS 1:4

_____

_____

Make the most of every opportunity in these evil days.
EPHESIANS 5:16

_____

_____

He has rescued us from the kingdom of darkness and transferred us into the Kingdom of his dear Son.
COLOSSIANS 1:13

_____

_____

To become a Christian is to be delivered from the power and authority of evil. But being a Christian doesn't mean we no longer have to face the evil that exists in the world around us. Nor does it mean we always access the authority we've been given in Christ to rule over this evil.

The Bible makes it clear that although Christ will ultimately win, for now this world lies under the power of evil. And Satan is specifically at work in those who walk in disobedience to Christ. Satan has the greatest freedom to work where the human will is most ready to defy the will of God.

And how exactly does Satan do this?

Let's unpack a few ways Satan tempts us to give in to the storms of life instead of fixing our eyes on Christ.

Read the following passages, looking for Satan's strategies.

Barnabas and Saul were sent out by the Holy Spirit. They went down to the seaport of Seleucia and then sailed for the island of Cyprus. There, in the town of Salamis, they went to the Jewish synagogues and preached the word of God. John Mark went with them as their assistant.

Afterward they traveled from town to town across the entire island until finally they reached Paphos, where they met a Jewish sorcerer, a false prophet named Bar-Jesus. He had attached himself to the governor, Sergius Paulus, who was an intelligent man. The governor invited Barnabas and Saul to visit him, for he wanted to hear the word of God. But Elymas, the sorcerer (as his name means in Greek), interfered and urged the governor to pay no attention to what Barnabas and Saul said. He was trying to keep the governor from believing.

Saul, also known as Paul, was filled with the Holy Spirit, and he looked the sorcerer in the eye. Then he said, "You son of the devil, full of every sort of deceit and fraud, and enemy of all that is good! Will you never stop perverting the true ways of the Lord? Watch now, for the Lord has laid his hand of punishment upon you, and you will be struck blind. You will not see the sunlight for some time." Instantly mist and darkness came over the man's eyes, and he began groping around begging for someone to take his hand and lead him.

When the governor saw what had happened, he became a believer, for he was astonished at the teaching about the Lord.

ACTS 13:4-12

What did Satan do in an attempt to hinder the governor's faith?

_____

_____

If the Good News we preach is hidden behind a veil, it is hidden only from people who are perishing. Satan, who is the god of this world, has blinded the minds of those who don't believe. They are unable to see the glorious light of the Good News. They don't understand this message about the glory of Christ, who is the exact likeness of God.

2 CORINTHIANS 4:3-4

How does Satan try to blind would-be believers?

_____

_____

[Jesus] told many stories in the form of parables, such as this one:

"Listen! A farmer went out to plant some seeds. As he scattered them across his field, some seeds fell on a footpath, and the birds came and ate them. . . . The seed that fell on the footpath represents those who hear the message about the Kingdom and don't understand it. Then the evil one comes and snatches away the seed that was planted in their hearts."

MATTHEW 13:3-4, 19

According to this parable, how does Satan try to prevent a person from believing?

_____

_____

What we are up against is a global power that touches and, in some measure, controls culture and society. Satan uses people to hinder faith; he blinds people to the truth. If we're going to remain standing in faith when the wind blows at our faces and the waves crash against us, we must learn to respond like Peter did when he started to sink.

Like Peter, all we need to do is cry, "Help!"

Day 5

Peter tends to catch a lot of haters from the "sinking incident."

Some people cast Peter as unfaithful and say he took his eyes off Jesus in a moment of weakness. But the Bible never says Peter took his eyes off Jesus; it simply says that "he saw the strong wind and the waves." I believe it's possible Peter never actually looked away from Jesus; he just noticed the course of events happening around him.

Most godly people don't wake up one day and set out to sin. But it's easy for us, no matter how faithful we are, to get distracted by the evil that is a part of the world around us.

For example, you're checking out your groceries at the register, and all around you is the opportunity to lust over the half-naked bodies on the magazine covers.

Or you're minding your own business in the office when your coworker rounds the corner blurting out the latest gossip.

Or you simply change the channel on your television and open up all kinds of opportunities to sin.

The point is, evil is part of our world, and we are surrounded by ample opportunities to choose sin over faith.

We see the wind and waves around us, just as Peter did.

I don't see Peter as someone who lacked faith. Instead, I see him as a believer of great faith—faith that begs us to follow his faithful yet watery footsteps.

So why is Peter an example of great faith? Because he's the only one who got out of the boat in the first place!

And while faith got Peter out of the boat, it was Jesus who kept his steps afloat. Peter knew that, which is why he didn't just jump out of the boat on his own.

Here are Peter's words to Jesus: "Lord, if it's really you, tell me to come to you, walking on the water" (Matthew 14:28).

Peter asked Jesus to tell him to come. Jesus honored Peter's faith by commanding the water to bear his weight.

Peter learned a significant faith lesson that day: real faith doesn't come from our ability to be faithful but from God's ability to be faithful.

And the storm was no accident. The purpose of the storm was to grow the faith of Peter and the other guys on the boat. Jesus knew he would leave them one day and they would face many storms without his physical presence to guide them. At some point they would most certainly wonder, *Where is Jesus when I need him?* Their own faith would never be enough to get them through those times, so Jesus wanted to teach them to depend completely on *his* faithfulness in the face of difficult circumstances.

Tell about a time when God grew your faith and dependence on him through a storm (a painful experience, a time of suffering, or a difficult trial).

_____

_____

When you were going through this storm, what made it difficult to stay focused on God's ability to be faithful to you? What helped you to stay focused on his faithfulness?

_____

_____

Peter learned another significant faith lesson through his water-walking experience: great faith happens when we come to the end of ourselves.

When he saw the strong wind and the waves, he was terrified and began to sink. "Save me, Lord!" he shouted.

MATTHEW 14:30

Complete surrender is the only way to go deeper in your faith. Peter knew this full well. His sinking brought him to a place of being done with himself. He could no longer look within himself for the answer; he was in trouble—really sinking. He quickly realized there was nothing he could do to save himself, so he put all his pride aside long enough to say, "Help!"

Describe the last time you cried out in humility to the Lord for help. How did you get to the end of yourself? How did you know there was nothing else to do but cry out to him?

_____

_____

This leads to a final faith lesson Peter learned through his experience: sometimes God lets us sink.

Developing a trust in God that trumps everything we are, think, feel, and do is a lifelong pursuit, and I've never found it to be an easy lesson.

This is why God, in his grace, planned specific faith-building exercises or storms for us to go through.

Jesus was capable of holding Peter up that day, but had Jesus never let him sink, Peter wouldn't have experienced such deep grace and love from his Savior. It was grace that allowed him to sink slowly instead of sinking quickly, like a stone in water. And it was love that allowed Peter to know that whatever storms he would face in the future, God would always be there—present and working out all things for his good.

Describe a time when God allowed you to "sink." In what ways did you experience God's love and grace through that process?

_____

_____

In the days to come, Peter would need to lean on the faith that had been tested when he got out of the boat.

Read the following verses to see what happened to Peter after he walked (and sank) on the water.

[Jesus said,] "Now I say to you that you are Peter (which means 'rock'), and upon this rock I will build my church, and all the powers of hell will not conquer it."

MATTHEW 16:18

As Simon Peter was standing by the fire warming himself, they asked him again, "You're not one of his disciples, are you?"

He denied it, saying, "No, I am not."

But one of the household slaves of the high priest, a relative of the man whose ear Peter had cut off, asked, "Didn't I see you out there in the olive grove with Jesus?" Again Peter denied it. And immediately a rooster crowed.
JOHN 18:25-27

Peter jumped up and ran to the tomb to look. Stooping, he peered in and saw the empty linen wrappings; then he went home again, wondering what had happened.
LUKE 24:12

Peter's words pierced their hearts, and they said to him and to the other apostles, "Brothers, what should we do?"

Peter replied, "Each of you must repent of your sins and turn to God, and be baptized in the name of Jesus Christ for the forgiveness of your sins. Then you will receive the gift of the Holy Spirit. This promise is to you, to your children, and to those far away—all who have been called by the Lord our God." Then Peter continued preaching for a long time, strongly urging all his listeners, "Save yourselves from this crooked generation!"

Those who believed what Peter said were baptized and added to the church that day—about 3,000 in all.
ACTS 2:37-41

Place a check next to the statements that are true about Peter's life based on the passages above.

☐ Peter played a vital role in establishing the church.
☐ Peter was blinded by a light on the road to Damascus.
☐ Peter wanted to see Jesus' empty tomb for himself.
☐ Peter helped Jesus carry his cross up Calvary's hill.
☐ Peter denied knowing Jesus.
☐ Peter became one of the first preachers to tell others the Good News.
☐ Peter baptized Jesus.

After his faith lesson on the water, Peter had highs and lows in his life. He would see the waves again and again in his lifetime, but he knew in the midst of it all that God's faithfulness remained rock solid, even when Peter's faith wasn't. Peter's life is a reminder to us that God gives us all we need when we need it—namely, his presence.

As God makes his presence known in the middle of the storms we weather, may we respond as the disciples did:

When they climbed back into the boat, the wind stopped. Then the disciples worshiped him. "You really are the Son of God!" they exclaimed.

MATTHEW 14:32-33

Questions for Group Discussion or Personal Reflection

1. The Bible says that Peter saw the waves when he was walking on the water. When have you seen the "waves" of distraction around you as you were walking toward Jesus?

_____

_____

2. When have your "waves" come in the form of temptations?

_____

_____

3. When have your "waves" come as rebellion and sin?

_____

_____

4. When have your "waves" come as suffering and trials?

_____

_____

5. Like Peter, when have you felt yourself facing doubts and sinking?

_____

_____

6. How do you think Peter felt when Jesus grabbed his hand and pulled him up out of the water?

_____

_____

7. Tell about a time when God pulled you out of the water of your doubts and fears.

_____

_____

8. How did this experience change your relationship with Jesus? How did it impact those around you?

_____

_____

9. Why is it difficult for us to place our faith in God and his promises when our feelings and circumstances tell us otherwise?

_____

_____

10. Read 1 John 3:20. What does it mean to you that God is greater than our feelings?

_____

_____

Week 6
....
The Raw Faith of Ruth

Ruth and her mother-in-law, Naomi, lived during one of the darkest, most rebellious periods in Israel's history. They were surrounded, as we are today, by people who were not believers. Unfortunately most of the Israelites at the time weren't living as salt and light to the watching world; instead, they were succumbing to the temptations around them.

Living in such a godless, wicked time, Ruth shines all the brighter as one of the few examples of obedience and loyalty in a world that desperately needed a picture of real faith.

In the Old Testament, famine in the land often came in direct correlation to God's judgment. This time was no exception. During the period of the judges, the people all did what was right in their own eyes instead of following God. This is the scene painted for us when we are introduced to Ruth's in-laws.

Because of the lack of food in the land, Naomi's husband, Elimelech, decided to relocate his family from Bethlehem to Moab. Their two sons, Mahlon and Kilion, went with them.

We are told that sometime after the family settled in Moab, Elimelech died. Naomi must have suffered greatly—first to be so far from home, and then to be left a widow. Her grief may have deepened even more over the fact that both of her sons married Moabite women.

Now let's look at the historical context for why intermarriage would have been heartbreaking for Naomi. God's chosen people, the Israelites, were strictly forbidden to marry those who didn't share their faith. Moabites didn't worship the one true God; they worshiped idols. That meant they were enemies of God and enemies of his chosen people. Despite the Lord's command, both Mahlon and Kilion married Moabite women—Orpah and Ruth. And in the ten years they lived in Moab, neither woman bore a child.

This family was most certainly in trouble. The father was dead, the mother was grieving, the sons were rebelling against God, and there were no heirs on the horizon.

Was there hope? Would there be redemption for those who hadn't followed the Lord's commands? Would there be a future beyond the pain and suffering this family had endured? And most important, what does this story have to say to us about faith?

Let's find out together. Welcome to our final week of digging in to raw faith.

Day 1

Naomi's circumstances were certainly stacked against her. When life is hard, all of us struggle to see that God is behind the scenes, working for our good. I encourage you to put yourself in Naomi's shoes as we study her story, feeling her pain and watching her embrace her blessings.

Read Ruth 1:4-5.

The two sons married Moabite women. One married a woman named Orpah, and the other a woman named Ruth. But about ten years later, both Mahlon and Kilion died. This left Naomi alone, without her two sons or her husband.

What tragedy befalls this family after the loss of Elimelech?

_____

_____

Who is left to care for Naomi?

_____

_____

This story is getting about as dark and hopeless as it can get!

Remember, the family's patriarch, Elimelech, originally moved his family to Moab so they would survive the famine. Yet within a span of ten years, all three men were dead (causes unknown).

I've been through my fair share of grief and suffering, but I can't think of anything more unbearable than experiencing the death of a child. As a mother, I find that unfathomable. As a human, I find it unjust. And as a believer, I'm convinced it's one of the greatest tests of faith known to humankind.

I want us to empathize with Naomi in this moment.

I want us to see her as a dear friend—perhaps a coworker, a neighbor, or someone from church.

What feelings do you imagine Naomi would have been going through during this time?

_____

_____

What questions do you think Naomi would have had for God?

_____

_____

Naomi was most assuredly at the end of herself. There she was—a widow who had buried both her children, living in the land of Moab where she had no place to worship, no extended family, and no godly friends to hug her, pray with her, and cry with her. And on top of that, she was most likely broke and hungry.

Read Ruth 1:6.

Naomi heard in Moab that the LORD had blessed his people in Judah by giving them good crops again. So Naomi and her daughters-in-law got ready to leave Moab to return to her homeland.

What does Naomi do next?

_____

_____

It was in the middle of tragic circumstances that Naomi's life was about to turn a corner.

Faith Anchor #1: With raw faith, we experience true blessing. Naomi heard a report that the famine in Bethlehem had ended, so she decided to return home. As a result, she was about to experience the blessing of living inside God's will.

Luke 15 tells the story of the Prodigal Son, who was also far from home and living outside his father's blessing. It wasn't until he was in the pigpen, longing to eat the pigs' food, that he realized how much he missed the blessings that could have been his.

Read Luke 15:17.

When he finally came to his senses, he said to himself, "At home even the hired servants have food enough to spare, and here I am dying of hunger!"

There is bread to spare where the Lord's will abides!

How sad it is when God's people only *hear* about God's blessing, when his desire is for us to *experience* it firsthand. He longs for us to taste the blessings that come when we follow his will. But when we start to disbelieve that the Lord is faithful, we depart from his will and find ourselves wandering in an "unblessable" region.

So what should we do if we sense that we have drifted away from God's will? That's when we must repent and return to the place of his blessing immediately—no matter how much it damages our pride, no matter how painful it might be to return. And we need to be careful to do it with the right heart.

Naomi decided to return to where God wanted her to be, but she did so with the wrong motive. Instead of trusting that the Lord was still at work, she was focused on her own bitterness. So while she did experience a measure of God's blessing, her bitterness kept her at arm's length from his full favor.

Things are far more bitter for me than for you, because the LORD himself has raised his fist against me.
RUTH 1:13

Naomi's decision was right, but her heart was in the wrong place. Instead of trusting God, she blamed him. She believed that the Lord was no longer worthy of her trust, and she gave up on the hope of having fellowship with him again.

Naomi was interested in returning to her land but not to her Lord.

What a powerful lesson for us.

Write about a time you changed direction or chose a new path—not because it would draw you closer to God, but because of what you would gain by doing so (for example, popularity, money, esteem, attention, a way to numb the pain, etc.).

_____

_____

_____

_____

What would it look like to truly surrender this part of your life to the Lord?

_____

_____

Our faith is most raw and vulnerable when we have wandered outside of the Lord's will. But these are also the moments God can use to shape our faith into something great and to bless us for trusting in him despite our pain and doubts.

Day 2

As we continue with Naomi's story, we come to an interesting twist—and one that doesn't do much for the often-joked-about mother-in-law stigma.

> Naomi heard in Moab that the LORD had blessed his people in Judah by giving them good crops again. So Naomi and her daughters-in-law got ready to leave Moab to return to her homeland. With her two daughters-in-law she set out from the place where she had been living, and they took the road that would lead them back to Judah.
> RUTH 1:6-7

Naomi's husband was dead, and she more than anyone would have been able to relate to Orpah and Ruth, who were also reeling from the grief of losing their husbands. So she made an empathetic mother-in-law move: she set off toward her homeland with her two widowed daughters-in-law.

The motive behind her departure may have been questionable, but her choice to take Orpah and Ruth with her to a land of godly influences and people who worshiped the one true God—now that was admirable.

But something happened along the way.

The Bible doesn't tell us if it was a few hours or weeks on the journey toward Judah, but at some point, Naomi changed her mind. She told Orpah and Ruth to go back to their homes in Moab. She essentially sent them off with a blessing and a wish that they'd find new husbands.

Wait a minute. What's going on here? It almost sounds like Naomi was pulling a martyr move in this passage, setting her daughters-in-law free so she wouldn't be a "burden" to them. But Naomi knew that if they stayed in Moab, they would remain stuck in their culture, worshiping idols. She should have been committed to bringing them to her homeland, where they'd experience genuine love and care from the one true God and his people. Why would she tell them to leave?

Faith Anchor #2: With raw faith, we will sometimes be uncomfortable. Have you ever been at what felt like a turning point in your relationship with God? Maybe you finally understood what that preacher was saying from the pulpit, or maybe that nagging feeling in your spirit to finally forgive wouldn't let you go. Perhaps you were reading the Bible one day and you suddenly realized it was no longer a burden—you were enjoying it. Or perhaps you knew beyond the shadow of a doubt that God was leading you to a new place or job or lifestyle.

Think back to a moment in your life when you knew a big faith move was just around the corner (transformation, liberation, insight, restoration, etc.). What was that moment like?

_____

_____

What emotions did you experience at the time (doubt, anticipation, fear, worry, skepticism, excitement, etc.)?

_____

_____

I think it's safe to say that somewhere deep within her, Naomi knew she was on the verge of something great with God. She was about to reconnect with her Lord—perhaps for the first time in a long time.

The truth is, experiencing raw faith can be uncomfortable because it brings our sin and disobedience into the light for others to see. As long as Naomi stayed in Moab, no one back home knew that her sons had disobeyed the Lord's command and united with Moabite women. As long as Naomi stayed in Moab, none of her "church friends" could speculate about her husband and sons and gossip about whether their deaths were a consequence of their disobedience. As long as Naomi stayed in Moab, she could stay comfortable.

This is one of the most difficult things we have to face in fighting for our faith—not simply owning our sin, but also letting people see it.

Everything inside us can know we're right where God wants us to be, yet we dread our friend's reaction, our mother's glare, or our spouse's rejection. The thought of being on the receiving end of other people's opinions and attitudes is often enough to keep us miserable in the land of Moab.

Naomi had one more test of faith to endure—going home.

Read John 8:2-11 for the story of someone else in Scripture who had to get uncomfortable in order to grow in her faith.

Early the next morning he was back again at the Temple. A crowd soon gathered, and he sat down and taught them. As he was speaking, the teachers of religious law and the Pharisees brought a woman who had been caught in the act of adultery. They put her in front of the crowd.

"Teacher," they said to Jesus, "this woman was caught in the act of adultery. The law of Moses says to stone her. What do you say?"

They were trying to trap him into saying something they could use against him, but Jesus stooped down and wrote in the dust with his finger. They kept demanding an answer, so he stood up again and said, "All right, but let the one who has never sinned throw the first stone!" Then he stooped down again and wrote in the dust.

When the accusers heard this, they slipped away one by one, beginning with the oldest, until only Jesus was left in the middle of the crowd with the woman. Then Jesus stood up again and said to the woman, "Where are your accusers? Didn't even one of them condemn you?"

"No, Lord," she said.

And Jesus said, "Neither do I. Go and sin no more."

Who are the key people in this story?

_____

_____

What did the woman in this story do wrong?

_____

_____

According to Mosaic law, what was the punishment for her sin?

_____

_____

How did Jesus respond to the Pharisees' accusations against this woman?

_____

_____

How did the accusers respond to Jesus' challenge?

_____

_____

What was Jesus' specific instruction to the woman after everyone else left?

_____

_____

We don't know what this woman faced after she went home. But we do know it must have been uncomfortable.

Jesus had removed her guilt, taking her sin and God's wrath upon himself. But he didn't change the past or remove the relational pain she had to go home to. Maybe her husband forgave her and they moved on, or maybe there was a messy divorce. Maybe her parents loved her through it, or maybe they disowned her. Maybe her friends rallied around her to pray for her and speak truth over her, or maybe everyone abandoned her.

However uncomfortable it was when she got back home, we do know one thing— this woman experienced a turning point in her relationship with her Savior.

She had been washed clean and set free. And in Jesus, she was made into a new creation. God now viewed her as if she had never sinned. Even the earthly consequences of her sin became a means of grace because God used them to bring her to himself.

God's grace was sufficient for this woman (just as it was sufficient for Naomi and Ruth, as we will soon see). His grace covers our sin when we are forced to go home and face our doubters and accusers.

Day 3

The Bible places great value on people of determination. Throughout Scripture, God frequently grants his favor on his children who show endurance, including our very own Ruth.

Read the verse below. Circle the text that represents Ruth's easy choice; underline the words that represent her difficult choice.

[Naomi] said, "See, your sister-in-law has gone back to her people and to her gods; return after your sister-in-law." But Ruth said, "Do not urge me to leave you or to return from following you. For where you go I will go, and where you lodge I will lodge. Your people shall be my people, and your God my God. Where you die I will die, and there will I be buried. May the LORD do so to me and more also if anything but death parts me from you." And when Naomi saw that she was determined to go with her, she said no more.

RUTH 1:15-18, ESV

Fill in the blank, based on the Scripture passage above.

"When Naomi saw that she was _____ to go with her, she said no more."

Sadly, the virtue of godly determination is difficult to come by in our culture. We are easily attracted to quick fixes, instant gratification, and "wow" moments that quickly fade away. It's a rare gift to encounter someone who remains persistent with God, enduring the heart-wrenching trials of life with faith.

Give some examples of quick fixes or instant gratification this world offers us (for example, drive-through restaurants; pay-at-the-pump gas stations; express checkouts at the grocery store).

_____

_____

Match each verse to what it says about endurance.

Luke 21:19	In death or captivity or persecution, we must endure.
Romans 5:4	We run our race with endurance.
2 Corinthians 6:4	By our endurance, we gain life and win our souls.
Hebrews 12:1	Endurance produces character.
Revelation 13:10	As servants of God, we must endure trouble with patience.

The book of Ruth was written not to record her outstanding talents, skills, or moments of fame. Her name will go down in history as a woman who endured in faith.

Faith Anchor #3: With raw faith, we endure. Ruth endured. She walked each day with God, steady and sure. Naomi was attempting to cover up, and Orpah had given up, but Ruth stood up!

Ruth refused to follow her sister-in-law's example of bailing, and she refused to listen to her mother-in-law's advice about turning back. Like each of these other women, Ruth had experienced trials, pain, grief, and disappointment, but instead of running away or blaming God, she trusted her heavenly Father.

Ruth allowed her suffering to strengthen her. This is true faith.

Raw, life-altering faith is not found in the sensational moments; it's found in daily endurance, in those ordinary days when nothing big or dramatic happens. God treasures the faith of those who keep walking with him and don't look back.

Ruth didn't look back. Perhaps she wanted to. Maybe everything in her was tugging at her to stay in Moab with her parents and the friends she'd grown up with. It certainly would have been easier. Moab was home; Moab was familiar.

But to stay would not have been to endure faithfully with God. To stay would have been to miss God's deep blessings.

Ruth chose God—not the quick fix or the path of least resistance. She chose faith.

And now Ruth's response to Naomi will forever be referenced as one of the most inspirational passages in all of Scripture.

Ruth replied, "Don't ask me to leave you and turn back. Wherever you go, I will go; wherever you live, I will live. Your people will be my people, and your God will be my God. Wherever you die, I will die, and there I will be buried. May the LORD punish me severely if I allow anything but death to separate us!"

RUTH 1:16-17

Rewrite this passage in the space below.

_____

_____

First, Ruth showed her love to Naomi and her desire to stay with her, even until death. Second, she showed her faith in the true God. Ruth was determined to endure despite the difficulties she was facing. And in this moment, God's grace wrote her into the history books of raw faith.

To conclude today's lesson, journal about an area of your life where you are currently showing endurance. In what ways are you remaining determined and consistent with God despite your circumstances? What (or who) is making it difficult for you to endure? What (or who) is encouraging you to keep going?

_____

_____

_____

_____

Day 4

Before God changes our circumstances, he wants to change our hearts.

If our circumstances get better while our hearts remain the same, we become prideful.

If our circumstances get worse while our hearts remain the same, we despair.

He wants our hearts more than anything else.

Read Romans 8:29.

God knew his people in advance, and he chose them to become like his Son, so that his Son would be the firstborn among many brothers and sisters.

What is God's ultimate goal when he deals with our hearts?

_____

_____

God's ultimate goal for us is that our hearts will come to reflect Jesus more and more. He wants us to surrender to him at all times so that our hearts will be directed toward his will.

Faith Anchor #4: With raw faith, God changes our hearts. Naomi was bitter toward God, but Ruth was willing to let God have his way in her life. In the remaining chapters of the book named after her, we see a brilliant and gracious plan unfold in her life. God's extreme love and grace rain down on his daughter Ruth for one reason: her raw and vulnerable faith in the one true God.

Read what happens when Naomi and Ruth return to Bethlehem.

When they came to Bethlehem, the entire town was excited by their arrival. "Is it really Naomi?" the women asked.

"Don't call me Naomi," she responded. "Instead, call me Mara, for the Almighty has made life very bitter for me. I went away full, but the Lord has brought me home empty. Why call me Naomi when the Lord has caused me to suffer and the Almighty has sent such tragedy upon me?"

So Naomi returned from Moab, accompanied by her daughter-in-law Ruth, the young Moabite woman. They arrived in Bethlehem in late spring, at the beginning of the barley harvest.

RUTH 1:19-22

How did Naomi describe her heart to the women in the community upon her return?

_____

_____

At what season did Naomi and Ruth return to Bethlehem?

_____

_____

Now there was a wealthy and influential man in Bethlehem named Boaz, who was a relative of Naomi's husband, Elimelech.

One day Ruth the Moabite said to Naomi, "Let me go out into the harvest fields to pick up the stalks of grain left behind by anyone who is kind enough to let me do it."

Naomi replied, "All right, my daughter, go ahead." So Ruth went out to gather grain behind the harvesters. And as it happened, she found herself working in a field that belonged to Boaz, the relative of her father-in-law, Elimelech.

While she was there, Boaz arrived from Bethlehem and greeted the harvesters. "The Lord be with you!" he said.

"The Lord bless you!" the harvesters replied.

Then Boaz asked his foreman, "Who is that young woman over there? Who does she belong to?"

And the foreman replied, "She is the young woman from Moab who came back with Naomi. She asked me this morning if she could gather grain behind the harvesters. She has been hard at work ever since, except for a few minutes' rest in the shelter."

RUTH 2:1-7

Did Boaz recognize Ruth?

_____

_____

What can we tell about Ruth's work ethic from this passage?

_____

_____

Boaz went over and said to Ruth, "Listen, my daughter. Stay right here with us when you gather grain; don't go to any other fields. Stay right behind the young women working in my field.

See which part of the field they are harvesting, and then follow them. I have warned the young men not to treat you roughly. And when you are thirsty, help yourself to the water they have drawn from the well."

Ruth fell at his feet and thanked him warmly. "What have I done to deserve such kindness?" she asked. "I am only a foreigner."

"Yes, I know," Boaz replied. "But I also know about everything you have done for your mother-in-law since the death of your husband. I have heard how you left your father and mother and your own land to live here among complete strangers. May the LORD, the God of Israel, under whose wings you have come to take refuge, reward you fully for what you have done."

RUTH 2:8-12

How did Boaz protect Ruth?

_____

_____

Why did Boaz treat Ruth with such kindness even though he didn't know her personally?

_____

_____

As Ruth was in the field all day—sweaty, dirty, and thirsty, with calluses beginning to develop on her hands from gathering grain—she had no idea that God was working behind the scenes to unfold his divine plan and purpose. His plan was far greater than the lives of Naomi, Ruth, and the husbands who had died. The Creator had had a supernatural design set up for their story long before he hung the stars in the sky.

Read Genesis 12:1-3 to see God's ultimate plan for his chosen people.

The Lord had said to Abram, "Leave your native country, your relatives, and your father's family, and go to the land that I will show you. I will make you into a great nation. I will bless you and make you famous, and you will be a blessing to others. I will bless those who bless you and curse those who treat you with contempt. All the families on earth will be blessed through you."

Rewrite God's big-picture plan in your own words.

_____

_____

Ruth's story began with the death of her husband, but it would end with the birth of a baby.

Ruth's circumstances changed drastically, but more important, so did her heart.

Ruth was the recipient of God's favor because of one thing: her heart was faithful to the God she knew little about and whom her own people didn't worship. Yet despite her unanswered questions about God and his call to her to leave her homeland and move into the unknown, Ruth lived out genuine faith. She endured even when it seemed that God was anything but faithful.

Make a list of the ways God seems to have been unfaithful to Ruth up to this point in her story.

_____

_____

Make a list of the ways God seems to have been unfaithful to you up to this point in your life.

_____

_____

It's important that we understand our own unanswered questions about God's faithfulness to us. Because this is the place where true faith can grow. To live by faith means to *believe God*, not simply to *believe in God*. Living by faith means taking God at his word even when he seems to be speaking few words to us. Living by faith means surrendering our hearts to God even when our circumstances tell us to become prideful or despairing. Living by faith means getting up and going to work in the field when it would be much easier to stay in bed under the covers.

As we watch the final chapter of Ruth's story unfold, we see the mighty hand of God at work in the least likely people and the least likely circumstances.

By the divine providence of God, Ruth went to work in a field that belonged to Boaz. This was no accident, for her footsteps were guided by God in faith. And the same is true for us. Even when it seems like God is silent, he is behind the scenes, writing a script that is much grander than we can imagine.

Day 5

As we learn in Ruth's story, God's grace flows through the channel of his promise, not his command. God's favor was on Ruth, not because she followed the rules, but because her heart sincerely wanted to follow God.

Faith Anchor #5: With raw faith, it's all about "I get to," not "I have to." The commands God lays out for believers show us his holiness and point out our own sinfulness. But that is all they are able to do. They cannot give us a heart to obey him through faith.

One of the greatest struggles facing believers and churches today is the "I have to" mentality.

When we feel that we owe God something, we do not have a heart of faith.

When we feel we must prove our goodness to God and others, we do not have a heart of faith.

When we feel that God is a God of rules and that he wants us to be perfect, we do not have a heart of faith.

Faithful hearts, like those of Ruth and Boaz, flow out of the promises of God, not the demands of God.

Read Romans 4:5.

People are counted as righteous, not because of their work, but because of their faith in God who forgives sinners.

What does this verse mean to you?

_____

_____

Without understanding and believing God's promises, we will never experience genuine faith. It is these promises that draw us near to his divine nature and give us the ability to get up and fight for another day.

Describe an area of your life where you are tempted to work for God's approval instead of walking in his promises.

_____

_____

When our hearts are dependent on the promises of our Father, we begin to function in the "I get to" realm of faith, which is the only kind of faith that honors God. In other words, our lives begin to look a little more like Ruth's.

I don't have to go to church; I get to go to church.
I don't have to respect my parents; I get to respect my parents.
I don't have to honor my boss; I get to honor my boss.

In what areas of your life do you need to switch from "I have to" to "I get to"? Write at least three of them below.

_____

_____

Boaz took Ruth into his home, and she became his wife. When he slept with her, the LORD enabled her to become pregnant, and she gave birth to a son. Then the women of the town said to Naomi, "Praise the LORD, who has now provided a redeemer for your family! May this child be famous in Israel. May he restore your youth and care for you in your old age. For he is the son of your daughter-in-law who loves you and has been better to you than seven sons!"

Naomi took the baby and cuddled him to her breast. And she cared for him as if he were her own. The neighbor women said, "Now at last Naomi has a son again!" And they named him Obed. He became the father of Jesse and the grandfather of David.

RUTH 4:13-17

What did Boaz and Ruth name their son?

_____

_____

Obed would later become whose father?

_____

_____

Obed would later become whose grandfather?

_____

_____

Read the last part of the genealogy recorded in Matthew 1:5-6, 16.

Jacob was the father of Joseph, the husband of Mary.
Mary gave birth to Jesus, who is called the Messiah.

Who would be the promised descendant of Boaz, Obed, Jesse, and David?

_____

_____

There is no better way to end this study than by pointing to the true hero, not only in Ruth's story, but in our stories as well: Jesus.

The book of Ruth reflects the love, grace, and blessing Jesus pours into our lives when we respond in unbridled faith.

Many people in Ruth's situation would have been content to simply stay in the comfort of their homeland, wasting away in the mire of doubt, worry, fear, and grief and viewing God as a condemning rule giver instead of a living Redeemer. But not Ruth.

God chose a broken widow who didn't know much about the true God as someone who would go down in history as part of the greatest lineage known to humankind—the lineage of the Savior of the world.

When we stay focused on our suffering, like Naomi, we become bitter and negative. But when we choose to see God's sanctifying work in our lives, as Ruth did, we get to serve him with joy and faithfulness.

Faith is the assurance of things hoped for, the conviction of things not seen.
HEBREWS 11:1, ESV

Faith is not about the present.

Faith is about the future promises of God—being certain that the will of God will happen no matter what our current circumstances look like.

It's time to get honest. What current circumstances are keeping you from believing that God is about to do something great in your life?

_____

_____

What do you think will happen if you genuinely yield your heart to God's promises for your future? How can you take one step toward surrender today?

_____

_____

What specific things need to change in your life in order for Jesus to become the hero of your story?

_____

_____

Once we've encountered the God who is worthy of our raw faith, may we never settle for anything less than a mighty move of God in our hearts. May our mediocre expectations be blown to smithereens as we allow these truths to sink deep into our hearts and minds.

Let us go right into the presence of God with sincere hearts fully trusting him. For our guilty consciences have been sprinkled with Christ's blood to make us clean, and our bodies have been washed with pure water. Let us hold tightly without wavering to the hope we affirm, for God can be trusted to keep his promise.
HEBREWS 10:22-23

Will you remain the same as you leave these pages? Or will you be moved toward a deeper place with Jesus?

In the bare places of our faith, God longs to usher us into his presence—his mighty, holy, forgiving, loving, gracious, and wise presence. A place where nothing stays the same except him.

And that, my friend, is where I choose to stay—raw before him, with a heart that stands naked, vulnerable, and exposed. No matter what I see around me or in front of me, I will cling to the belief that God has a divine plan and promise.

Will you stand in that place with me?

I beg you, dear one—join me. For there is no life worth living other than that of raw faith.

Questions for Group Discussion or Personal Reflection

1. Do you find it hard to trust God sometimes, even when you know his promises?

_____

_____

2. Read Psalm 51:10-12. What does David ask of God in this passage?

_____

_____

3. According to this passage, how can we get a loyal or steadfast spirit? How can we obtain a willing spirit to do whatever God asks us to do?

_____

_____

4. What happens when we try to do God's will on our own rather than depending on his Holy Spirit to work from within us?

_____

_____

5. After studying Ruth this week, how would you describe her faith?

_____

_____

6. Is your faith a Ruth-like faith? If not, what might be keeping you from walking in faith and joy according to God's plan?

_____

_____

7. The Bible says that God "has given us great and precious promises. These are the promises that enable you to share his divine nature and escape the world's corruption caused by human desires" (2 Peter 1:4). What makes God's promises great and precious?

_____

_____

8. If we don't feed on the promises in God's Word, what will happen to us? Why?

_____

_____

9. What happens when we believe our faithful God has the power to completely change our lives?

_____

_____

10. Think of some parts of your life that are not yet the way God wants them to be. What is keeping you from embracing his promises and letting him do his work in these areas?

_____

_____

Leader's Guide

So, you have taken on the bittersweet task of facilitating a small group Bible study. Although some of you who carry the title "group leader" do so with your crowns firmly in place, propped up by years of positive experience, others of you may be feeling your crown drooping a little toward the back. You may even feel like you've forgotten your crown at home under the hamper loads of laundry and sink full of dirty dishes. In fact, you might find yourself as the reigning Ms. Small Group Leader only because you chose to scratch your back at the exact moment the director called for volunteers!

Several years ago, I must have scratched my back at the wrong time during a women's ministry planning meeting at my home church, because I found myself stuttering and stammering through a twelve-week small group study as the facilitator of fifteen ladies, all of whom were five years or more my elder. I remember breaking out in hives before each session and breaking down in sobs after each session. I found myself doubting everything about my ability to lead a group made of (big gulp) Christians! I didn't feel mature enough, experienced enough, knowledgeable enough, and certainly not righteous enough to hold such a title, yet it seemed the Lord had seen fit to shove me out of my snug and cozy comfort zone.

Since I sensed the Lord's hand in this, I made a commitment to see the study through as group leader. Yes, I made mistakes—many of them!—and my group fluctuated in number, dwindling to only five participants during our final weeks together. I had brain freezes and tongue twists on a regular basis. I didn't know most of the answers to the participants' questions, and one time I even came prepared for the wrong week's study! However, something else—a *great* something else—happened through those twelve weeks of unintended leadership: I found myself completely reliant on the Lord for one of the first times in my life!

Whether you are a seasoned veteran in the world of group leadership or are finding yourself stepping up for the first time, I'm honored to extend my gratitude and admiration to you, child of the King. Be encouraged that your Father does not need your experience or wisdom to claim the victory for his purposes; he desires only your willingness. In fact, it is within your moments of complete loss that he is able to be your complete everything!

Throughout this six-week journey, I pray that you will sense me encouraging you on and that the Lord's supernatural filling will give you strength and confidence. Take heart "because of your partnership in the gospel from the first day until now, being confident of this, that he who began a good work in you will carry it on to completion until the day of Christ Jesus" (Philippians 1:5-6, NIV).

Stay committed. Stay intentional. Stay on your knees. Oh yeah, and have fun!

All my love,
Kasey

Recommended Resources for Leaders

1. Your Own Bible

For both the group sessions and your individual preparation time, you will need a Bible you are comfortable reading. Don't stress about the translation—it doesn't have to be the same as mine or the other participants' Bibles in your group. Just bring a Bible you feel drawn to and one you can understand easily. I will primarily be using the New Living Translation (NLT) in the study. Some of my faves are the NLT, the English Standard Version (ESV), the New International Version (NIV), and the New American Standard Bible (NASB). If you don't have a Bible, get one! If cost is a factor, talk to your church and see if they can help you out.

2. *Raw Faith* Book

If you're interested in taking this experience to a whole new, supernatural level, I encourage you to add one additional tool—*Raw Faith*, the book. This book was written to be read alongside the Bible study. Within the book I go deeper into my own story—my own painful experiences, my struggles with faith, and my doubts—as well as the breakthroughs I experienced along the way. I also dig into Scripture to follow people from the Bible and explore how God used their journeys of brokenness and raw faith to bring hope and purpose into their lives. It may be helpful for you as a leader to read the book as another way to connect with the other participants in your group.

3. Other Resources

I recommend that you have a pen and a journal handy as you do this study. Of course, you are welcome to write directly in the book, but if you're like me, you might write all over the lines and white space and still need more.

I'd also recommend that you invest in a good commentary. This will give you additional insights and background into the selected Scripture verses and help you with tricky passages you may encounter. I have found Logos Bible Software to be helpful in my own study and research. You can learn more about this electronic Bible study library at www.logos.com.

Oh, and you might need tissues at some point too. (My previous participants asked me to include this one for you!)

Group Tips

A small group can be an ideal setting for fellowship and accountability, as well as personal growth. Here are a few tips to help your group run as efficiently as possible and to maximize your time together.

A Few Logistics

- The ideal size for a discussion group is twelve people or fewer. However, I realize that is not always feasible. If you have a larger group, you will need to be creative and intentional about your discussion time. My suggestion would be to open with one general question, such as, "What truth most spoke to your heart this week, and why?" Then invite participants to share—either with the entire group or with the people at their table. You'll have to watch the clock carefully and let members know how much time is allotted for group discussion.
- If possible, plan for at least two hours of group time each week. This will allow for adequate time to discuss the questions and have some time for fellowship.
- Child care is highly recommended. Ask your child care workers to arrive fifteen minutes prior to each session to make sure the group can start on time.
- As the leader, you should arrive fifteen minutes prior to each session. Encourage participants to arrive promptly to maximize your time together.

Setting the Tone

If you have a group of twelve or fewer, set aside a little time at the beginning (ten minutes or so) for informal fellowship and a prayer by the group leader. If you have a larger group, you might consider a welcome from the director, a brief time of worship, and an introductory prayer before beginning the study.

What to Discuss

The Questions for Group Discussion or Personal Reflection at the end of each week can be used to facilitate discussion within your group. I encourage you to select certain Scripture passages and questions from the daily devotions to discuss as a whole group. Depending on the dynamics of your group, you may also want to ask participants to share what stood out to them from their individual study.

Closing Your Time Together

At the end of the session, encourage participants to complete their personal Bible study time and to come back next week. Take time to share prayer requests, and have one volunteer from the group record them and send them out in a group e-mail so participants can pray for one another throughout the week. Wrap up in a final prayer, asking that the Holy Spirit will do a life-transforming work within each participant.

Dealing with Problems

In dealing with any type of group, challenges are bound to arise. The most important thing you can do as a leader is to ask God for wisdom and discernment as you lead. Following are tips on how to deal with a few of the common problems small group leaders face.

- If a participant frequently misses sessions, show her you care. Call, e-mail, or write a note letting her know her presence is valued, desired, and missed.
- If participants are not completing their individual study time, stress to them that engaging in both the Bible study and the group time will help them get the most out of this experience. If they miss out on the Bible study, they are depriving themselves of the full impact of God's Word and its potential to bring complete transformation to their lives.
- If participants are getting into debates over certain issues, allow God's Word to be the final authority. Don't be scared of all disagreements—some debate is healthy and beneficial for growth. But if the argument is becoming unproductive or taking away from the unity of the group, gently ask the participants involved to meet with you one-on-one to discuss the matter further.

- If a participant is sharing "prayer requests" that are actually pieces of gossip, it is best to address the problem early. You want to be careful not to call someone out in front of the group in an embarrassing or devaluing way, but it is appropriate to interject a question such as, "Maria, how can we pray for you in this situation?" I also recommend that you arrange for a private conversation with the person outside the larger group. Make sure you approach situations like this with prayer and sensitivity.

- If participants are "oversharing" during prayer request time, you might want to set a time limit. You don't need to cut people off mid-sentence, but you can lovingly remind the group to keep their requests brief out of fairness to the other members. If you have a large group, the most effective tactic for prayer requests is to have members write out their prayer requests on note cards rather than sharing them out loud. At the end of the group session, each member can take the card of another member and pray for that request until the next meeting.

- If participants are dealing with concerns that require professional help, such as drug or alcohol abuse, sexual or physical abuse, or mental illness, do not try to take on those issues yourself. The best way to help in such situations is to pray with these individuals and to recommend that they see a Bible-based counselor in your area. In fact, I suggest that you research Christian counselors in your area prior to your first meeting and have a few note cards made up with their contact information so you'll be prepared.

Leader Tips

As the leader of your group, you have the privilege of taking the other members by the hand as they learn about God's Word and as God works in their hearts and lives. This is a big responsibility—one not to be taken lightly. Here are some tips to help you make the most of your role.

Plan Ahead

Talk with others in your church or community to find out about their Bible study needs and desires. Would they prefer that group sessions be held during the day or in the evening? Determine if child care is needed, and then investigate your options.

Advertise the Bible study in your church and community. You might start by making announcements at church, putting up flyers, and promoting it by word of mouth and through social media. If you are doing this study at your church, ask your pastor to endorse it on a Sunday morning. Participants will see that the church leadership values this study as an opportunity for group members to become more intimate in their relationship with Jesus and to build meaningful relationships with others in the church body.

Estimate the number of participants, and order your Bible study workbooks at least four weeks in advance. Determine whether the participants or the church will pay for the Bible study. (I've found that when participants invest financially in a study, they are more likely to attend and complete it.)

Reserve the room for the group sessions each week. If possible, make sure the meeting spot is the same every time.

Finally, pray that God will bring the participants of his choosing to this study. He knows exactly who needs this study at this time in their lives and what your group dynamics need to be.

Stay on Schedule

Do your best to start and end at the specified times for this study. Avoid chasing rabbit trails by steering participants toward new questions. It is critical for you to run a tight ship when it comes to the schedule—out of respect for your group members, who have other obligations outside of this time, and also out of respect for the facility you are using, which must be cleaned and reorganized after your group session ends.

Learn to Appreciate Silence

As the group leader, you may find yourself panicked by only a few seconds of silence. But do not allow the quiet to scare you! Simply wait a few moments after a question has been posed. If no one answers, rephrase the question, ask a different question, or call on someone you feel would be comfortable answering. Avoid answering your own questions.

Be Affirming

Remind your group that there are no dumb questions and no dumb answers. Develop your group as a safe zone, and remind participants that what is said within the group stays within the group. Be encouraging even when the answers are not what you expected or desired. Communicate how much you appreciate each person's participation. Be careful not to come across as judgmental of or shocked by a participant's response.

Know the Traps to Avoid

Be careful about using phrases like "I know just how you feel" or "It will be okay" when someone shares something with the group. The reality is, you probably do not understand the exact situation, and things might not be okay for the individual at that moment. These responses only make the person feel misunderstood and devalued.

Avoid giving your personal opinion based on your own experiences. It is certainly good for you to be open, honest, and vulnerable as a group leader, but never presume to make a sweeping generalization based only on your life.

Avoid talking at great lengths about yourself. Although your personal struggles, victories, revelations, and insights are valuable and should be discussed when appropriate, remember that your role as the leader is to facilitate the conversation of the whole group, not to dominate the time for your own venting or reminiscing.

Avoid the temptation to think it's your job to be someone's savior or counselor.

Before Jesus left his disciples, he assured them that the Father would send another Counselor—the Holy Spirit. "When the Father sends the Advocate as my representative—that is, the Holy Spirit—he will teach you everything and will remind you of everything I have told you" (John 14:26).

The Holy Spirit is the only one truly capable of guiding, instructing, rebuking, convicting, encouraging, and teaching God's Word. Your job is to point the members of your group to God and let him do the transformational work inside them.

Know the Things You Should Do

Remain confident in your God-given gifts and abilities. Although you may not be called to the position of pastor, counselor, or teacher, you are certainly capable of showing God's love and grace to other human beings. Embrace the person God has created you to be!

Allow the Word of God to have the final say. If a participant poses a question that you are unsure about, do not feel pressure to have the answer (or make one up!). Simply say, "I will commit to find that answer in Scripture and will get back to you next week." (You might consider e-mailing the answer with corresponding Scripture passages before the next group time to avoid backtracking.)

Stay committed to and focused on the Bible and resources that go along with it. As a leader, you are not expected to be a Bible scholar—only a Bible pursuer. The members of your group will benefit not only from your biblical knowledge as you go deeper in God's Word but also from your passion and love for God's Word.

Remain in continual prayer for the mighty movement of God in your group. Pray each week for soft hearts, gentle spirits, grace-filled words, loving communication, and the indwelling of the Holy Spirit. Banish Satan from each group time. Boldly ask the Lord to allow his supernatural work to take root in each participant's life—and in your own.

About the Author

Kasey Van Norman is a bestselling author and nationally known Bible teacher. Her breakout book and Bible study series, *Named by God*, gained national attention as an inspiring and cutting-edge journey into the redemptive power of Jesus through our past, present, and future.

In 2012, Kasey joined America's most explosive Christian women's movement, Extraordinary Women Conferences, as a headline speaker (www.ewomen.net). From 2012 to 2013, Kasey spoke to more than one hundred thousand women in North America about how God has redeemed her life as one of the least deserving people on the planet. Kasey uses her story to ignite a flame of passion in the hearts of believers and unbelievers alike.

Kasey is a licensed professional counselor who has earned degrees in psychology, public speaking, counseling, and biblical studies. She and her family currently live and work on a 280-acre rescue ranch in Central Texas called Still Creek Ranch, the only long-term care facility for sex-trafficked and severely abused/neglected children in the United States. Kasey's husband works as director of the equestrian program for the ranch while Kasey is acting director of counseling. To learn more about taking kids from crisis to new creation, check out www.still-creek.org.

Kasey is the founder and president of Kasey Van Norman Ministries (KVM), located in College Station, Texas. She is married to her best friend, Justin, and they have two children: Emma Grace and Lake. They are also the acting relief parents for the thirty-plus resident children at the ranch.

You are invited to discover your
true identity by drawing closer
to the one who named you!

Join **Kasey Van Norman** in pursuit of
what it means to be truly *Named by God*!

Named by God: Women of all ages will be able to connect with Kasey as she shares her story of God's infinite grace and compassion. As you journey with Kasey through Scripture and her personal experiences, you'll grow in your relationship with God.

Named by God Bible Study: Join Kasey as she leads you on a six-week journey of transformation! This interactive study will equip you to move beyond past hurts, bring power into your present circumstances, and ignite a victorious faith for your future.

Named by God Leader's Guide: As Kasey shares personal stories and directs you toward a more intimate relationship with Jesus Christ, this leader's guide will equip you to facilitate a life-changing journey through God's Word.

Named by God Video Curriculum: Join Kasey on this life-transforming journey by adding her six-session DVD curriculum to your personal or group study of *Named by God*.

CP0529